STUDY GUIDE
TO ACCOMPANY

PRINCIPLES OF FOOD, BEVERAGE, AND LABOR COST CONTROLS
NINTH EDITION

Paul R. Dittmer and J. Desmond Keefe III

WILEY

JOHN WILEY & SONS, INC.

Published by John Wiley and Sons, Inc., Hoboken, New Jersey.

Published simultaneously in Canada.

For general information on our other products and services, or technical support, please contact our Customer Care Department within the United States at 800-762-2974, outside the United States at 317-572-3993 or fax 317-572-4002.
Wiley also publishes its books in a variety of electronic formats. Some content that appears in print may not be available in electronic books. For more information about Wiley products, visit our Web site at http://www.wiley.com.

This material may be reproduced for testing or instructional purposes by instructors using the text, *Food, Beverage, and Labor Cost Controls, Ninth Edition* by Paul R. Dittmer and J. Desmond Keefe, III. (ISBN: 978-0471-78347-3).

For more information about Wiley products, visit our Web site at http://www.wiley.com.

Library of Congress Cataloging-in-Publication Data:

ISBN: 978-0470-14056-7

Printed in the United States of America

V10007037_122018

Table of Contents

To the Student:

The organization of each chapter in the Student guide is as follows:

I. LEARNING OBJECTIVES
This section will help you focus in on the important points discussed in the chapter.

II. CHAPTER OUTLINE
The purpose of the outline is to help you organize the chapter's main topics. It is also designed to allow you to write key points about each topic in the blank spaces provided.

III. KEY IDEAS
This is a summary of the important points discussed in the chapter.

IV. KEY TERMS
It is very important to know the terms and their definitions from each chapter so you can use them correctly in discussions and in further reading and study.

V. SELF-TEST
The self-test consists of matching, multiple choice, and essay questions. Use these to prepare yourself for exams administered by your instructor.

Here are some ideas for getting the optimum benefit from this student guide and the course.
- Read each chapter before attending class on the chapter being studied.
- Take brief concise notes in the chapter outline.
- Review the key ideas.
- Write out the definitions for the key terms.
- Take good notes in class.
- Complete any assignments given by your instructor, such as the end of chapter questions and problems or the spreadsheet exercises found on the accompanying CD-ROM.
- Review the chapter outline, key ideas and key terms in your student guide before taking an exam. You should also do the self-test for each chapter you are being tested on as a review.

Chapter 1
COST AND SALES CONCEPTS

I. LEARNING OBJECTIVES

Refer to these learning objectives while you are reading the chapter. They will help you focus in on the important points discussed in the chapter. Think of the learning objectives as questions that you will answer while reading the chapter.

1. Define the terms cost and sales.
2. Define and provide an example of the following types of costs: fixed, directly variable, semivariable, controllable, noncontrollable, unit, total, prime, historical, and planned.
3. Provide several examples illustrating monetary and nonmonetary sales concepts.
4. Describe the significance of cost-to-sales relationships and identify several cost-to-sales ratios important in food and beverage management.
5. Identify the formulas used to compute cost percent and sales price.
6. Describe factors that cause industrywide variations in cost percentages.
7. Explain the value of comparing current cost-to-sales ratios with those for previous periods.

II. CHAPTER OUTLINE

Following are the key headings from this chapter. The purpose of this outline is to help you organize the chapter's main topics. It is also designed to allow you to write key points about each topic in the blank spaces provided. While you are reading the chapter, be sure to take notes using this outline and you will certainly gain a better understanding of the chapter.

1. Introduction

      A. A Taste of Tuscany

      B. The Grandview Bistro

2. Cost Concepts

      A. Definition of Cost

      B. Fixed and Variable Costs

      C. Controllable and Noncontrollable Costs

      D. Unit and Total Costs

      E. Prime Cost

F. Historical and Planned Costs

3. Sales Concepts

    A. Sales Defined

    B. Monetary Terms

- Total Sales

      o By Category

         ▪ By Server

         ▪ By Seat

         ▪ Sales Price

         ▪ Average Sale

         ▪ Per Customer

         ▪ Per Server

    C. Nonmonetary Terms

- Total Number Sold

- Covers

- Total Covers

- Average Covers

- Seat Turnover

- Sales Mix

4. The Cost-To-Sales Ratio: Cost Percent

5. Industrywide Variations in Cost

6. Monitoring Costs and Sales

III. KEY IDEAS

1. Cost is defined as the expense to a hotel or restaurant of goods or services when the goods are consumed or the services rendered. **Sales** is defined as revenue resulting from the exchange of products and services for value. Food and beverage sales are exchanges of the products and services of a restaurant, bar, or related enterprise for value.

2. There are various types of costs. **Fixed costs** are those that are normally unaffected by changes in sales volume. **Variable costs** are those that are clearly related to business volume. **Directly variable costs** are those that are directly linked to volume of business, such that every increase or decrease in volume brings a corresponding increase or decrease in cost. **Semivariable costs** have both fixed and variable elements.

Controllable costs are those that can be changed in the short term. **Variable costs** are normally controllable. **Noncontrollable costs** are those that cannot normally be changed in the short term. These are usually fixed costs.

Unit costs may be food or beverage portions or units of work. **Total costs** may be the total cost of labor for one period.

Prime cost is the sum of food costs, beverage costs, and labor costs (salaries and wages, plus employee benefits). **Historical costs** can be found in business records, books of account, and other similar records. **Planned costs** are projections of what costs will be or should be for a future period.

3. There are two basic groups of terms normally used in food and beverage operations to express sales concepts: monetary and nonmonetary.

Monetary terms include total sales (total volume of sales expressed in dollar terms). **Total sales** may be given by category (such as total food sales or total beverage sales), by server (total dollar sales for which a given server has been responsible in a given time period), or by seat (total dollar sales for a given time period divided by the number of seats in the restaurant). Other monetary terms include sales price, average sale per customer (the result of dividing total dollar sales by the number of sales or customers), average sales per server(total dollar sales for a server divided by the number of customers served by that server).

Nonmonetary terms include total number sold (such as number of steaks sold in a given time period) and covers (one diner). Total covers refers to the total number of customers served in a given period. An average number of covers is determined by dividing the total number of covers for a given time period by some other number, such as number of hours of operation (this results in covers per hour) or number of servers (this results in covers per server). Other nonmonetary terms include seat turnover (the number of seats occupied during a given period divided by the number of seats) and sales mix (a term that describes the relative quantity sold of any menu item compared to other items in the same category).

4. Foodservice managers calculate costs in dollars and compare those costs to sales in dollars. This enables them to discuss the relationship between costs and sales, called the cost-to-sales ratio. The

3

following formula is used for calculating cost-to-sales ratio.

$$\frac{\text{Cost}}{\text{Sales}} = \text{Cost per Dollar of Sale or Cost \%}$$

The formula can be extended to show the following relationships.

$$\frac{\text{Food Cost}}{\text{Food Sales}} = \text{Food Cost \%}$$

$$\frac{\text{Beverage Cost}}{\text{Beverage Sales}} = \text{Beverage Cost \%}$$

$$\frac{\text{Labor Costs}}{\text{Total Sales}} = \text{Labor Cost \%}$$

Cost percents are useful to managers in at least two ways. They provide a means of comparing costs relative to sales for two or more periods of time, and they provide a means of comparing two or more operations.

5. The cost percent formula can be rearranged algebraically to facilitate other calculations. The calculation of a sales price is simplified if the formula is rearranged in the following form.

$$\frac{\text{Cost}}{\text{Cost \%}} = \text{Sales or Sales Price}$$

The calculation of cost is facilitated by rearranging the formula once again.

$$\text{Sales x Cost \%} = \text{Cost}$$

6. Cost percents vary considerably from one foodservice operation to another. There are many possible reasons for these variations: type of service, location, price structure, and type of menu.

7. It is very important to compare current cost-to-sales ratios with those for previous periods to see if the ratios are satisfactory. If not, remedial steps must be taken to bring these ratios into line with ratios from previous periods. Establishments that gather cost and sales information only monthly, quarterly, or annually may not be able to take effective remedial action because the information is not sufficiently timely to shed light on current problems. Total sales must exceed total costs if a foodservice enterprise is to be profitable.

IV. KEY TERMS

Following are the key terms discussed in the chapter. It is very important to know these terms and their definitions so you can use them correctly in discussions and in further reading and study. Use the blank spaces to write in definitions.

4

Average sale per customer

Average sale per server

Beverage cost

Budgeted cost

Controllable cost

Cost

Cost per dollar sale

Cost percent

Cover

Directly variable cost

Fixed cost

Food cost

Historical cost

Labor cost

Noncontrollable cost

Overhead

Planned cost

Prime cost

Sale

Sales mix

Sales price

Seat turnover

Semivariable cost

Total cost

Total sales

Total sales per seat

Unit cost

Variable cost

V. SELF-TEST

<u>MATCHING</u>

	TERMS	DEFINITIONS
_____ 1.	Cover	a. A cost that changes when sales volume changes.
_____ 2.	Fixed cost	b. The ratio of the number of sales of one menu item to the total number of all items.
_____ 3.	Variable cost	c. A diner

_____ 4.	Historical cost	d. The number of seats occupied during a given period divided by the total number of seats.
_____ 5.	Planned cost	e. The cost of one of many like units.
_____ 6.	Seat turnover	f. A past cost that has been documented in business records.
_____ 7.	Prime cost	g. A cost that management cannot change in the short term.
_____ 8.	Sales mix	h. The sum of food cost, beverage cost, and labor cost for a given operating period.
_____ 9.	Noncontrollable cost	i. An anticipated cost.
_____ 10.	Unit cost	j. A cost that is normally not affected by changes in sales volume.

MULTIPLE CHOICE

11. Beverage cost is incurred when the beverage is:
a. purchased by the foodservice.
b. issued by the foodservice.
c. purchased by the customer.
d. budgeted.

12. Which of the following is a fixed cost?
a. food
b. insurance premiums
c. labor
d. beverage

13. Controllable costs are usually:
a. fixed costs
b. unit costs
c. variable costs
d. prime costs

14. Which is the simplified version of the formula commonly used to determine cost percentage?
a. $\dfrac{Cost}{Covers\ served} = Cost\ \%$
b. $\dfrac{Sales}{Cost} = Cost\ \%$
c. $\dfrac{Profit}{Cost} = Cost\ \%$
d. $\dfrac{Cost}{Sales} = Cost\ \%$

15. If food cost percent is 40 percent, this means that 40 percent of the income from food sales has gone to cover:
a. food
b. labor
c. overhead
d. all of the above

16. Variations in cost percents from one foodservice operation to another may be due to:
a. type of service
b. location
c. price structure
d. all of the above

17. If 150 persons were served dinner in a dining room with 50 seats, seat turnover would be calculated as:
a. 0.33
b. 2
c. 3
d. 3.5

18. If 400 portions of prime rib sell during the first week of June, and total entrees sold was 2,000, what is the sales mix for prime rib?
a. 5 percent
b. 10 percent
c. 15 percent
d. 20 percent

19. If a restaurant's total sales on a given day were $2,000, and the restaurant had served 200 customers, what is the average dollar sale?

a. $1.00
b. $2.00
c. $10.00
d. $11.00

20. Average covers per hour is calculated by dividing total covers by the number of:
a. food and beverage items sold
b. hours of operation
c. servers
d. customers

ESSAY/PROBLEMS

21. Given the following information, calculate cost percentages to the nearest tenth of a percent.

Cost	Sales	Cost Percent
$250.00	$890.00	
$412.00	$1,300.00	

22. Calculate sales prices for the following items given the following figures for cost and desired cost percent.

Cost Percent	Cost	Sales Price
30%	Broiled Half-Chicken $1.90	
40%	Baked Salmon $2.75	

23. Explain why a comparison of food cost (or beverage cost or labor cost) percents of two restaurants would be more revealing than simply comparing dollar costs.

24. Given the following information, do the following calculations.

For one 3 hour dinner period: Number of seats: 150

Server	Covers	Gross Sales
A	75	$675.90
B	68	$646.40
C	79	$711.10
Total sales for dinner.		
Number of covers.		
Covers per hour.		
Covers per server.		
Average sale per customer.		
Average sale for server A.		
Number of Turns.		

25. Set up a statement of income with the following categories.

        Controllable Expenses
        Income Before Occupancy Costs, Interest, Depreciation, and
        Income Taxes
        Cost of Sales
        Sales
        Restaurant Profit
        Depreciation
        Gross Profit
        Interest Expense
        Income Before Interest, Depreciation, and Income Taxes
        Occupancy Costs

Chapter 2
THE CONTROL PROCESS

I. LEARNING OBJECTIVES

Refer to these learning objectives while you are reading the chapter. They will help you focus in on the important points discussed in the chapter. Think of the learning objectives as questions that you will answer while reading the chapter.

1. Define control and provide examples of its significance in food and beverage management.

2. Pinpoint responsibility for control in food and beverage operations.

3. Cite eight control techniques used in food and beverage operations.

4. Describe the steps involved in preparing an operating budget.

5. List the four steps in the control process.

6. Prepare a budget given fixed and variable costs for a restaurant.

7. Explain why the cost/benefit ratio is significant when making control decisions.

II. CHAPTER OUTLINE

Following are the key headings from this chapter. The purpose of this outline is to help you organize the chapter's main topics. It is also designed to allow you to write key points about each topic in the blank spaces provided. While you are reading the chapter, be sure to take notes using this outline and you will certainly gain a better understanding of the chapter.

1. Introduction

2. Definition of Control

3. Cost Control Defined

4. Sales Control

5. Responsibility for Control

6. Instituting Control

7. Control Techniques

        A. Establishing Standards

        B. Establishing Procedures

        C. Training

        D. Setting Examples

      E. Observing and Correcting Employee Actions

      F. Requiring Records and Reports

        G. Disciplining Employees

        H. Preparing and Following Budgets

8. The Control Process

9. Control Systems

10. Cost/Benefit Ratio

III. KEY IDEAS

1. Control is a process used by managers to direct, regulate, and restrain the actions of people so that the established goals of an enterprise may be achieved. Cost control is the process used by managers to regulate costs and guard against excessive costs. While cost control is critically important to the profitable operation of any business, cost control alone will not ensure profitability. Additional steps must be taken to ensure that all sales result in appropriate income to the business. Sales control is therefore also important.

2. Responsibility for every aspect of any food and beverage enterprise rests with management. In probably the majority of food and beverage enterprises, managers take personal charge of directing and supervising the control procedures in every phase of operations.

3. Control techniques available to a manager include the following.

    - Establishing standards

    - Establishing procedures

    - Training

    - Setting examples

      - Observing and correcting employee actions

    - Requiring records and reports

    - Disciplining employees

    - Preparing and following budgets

4. An operating budget is a forecast of sales activity and an estimate of costs that will be incurred

in the process of generating those sales. It is normally prepared using historical information from previous budgets and other financial records. This information, together with anticipated changes in sales and costs, provides the basic data needed to prepare an operating budget for an upcoming period. Typically an operating budget is developed for one full year and then broken down into smaller time units, such as quarters or months. A static budget assume only one level of business activity.

The initial step in the budgeting process is to examine sales figures from the recent past to note evident trends. The next step is to examine the external environment and assess any conditions or factors that could affect sales volume in the coming year. These would include general economic conditions in the nation and in the immediate geographical area, population changes, or changes that could affect transportation to the establishment. Another important step is to review any planned changes in the operation that would affect sales volume, such as changing menu prices.

The next logical step is to determine the nature and extent of changes in cost levels, some of which will be dictated by anticipated changes in sales volume and others of which will occur independent of volume changes. When projections for sales, costs, and profits are completed, they must be accepted by management in order to be adopted as the plan of action for the covered period. Once accepted, an operating budget become a standard against which operating performance is measured as the fiscal year progresses.

To counteract the inherent shortcomings of fixed operating budgets, a manager can prepare a budget designed to project sales and costs for several levels of business activity - a flexible budget.

5. The control process consists of four steps.

> - Establish standards and standard procedures for operation.

> - Train all individuals to follow established standards and standard procedures.

> - Monitor performance and compare actual performances with established standards.

> - Take appropriate action to correct deviations from standards.

6. The cost/benefit ratio is the relationship between the costs incurred in instituting and maintaining a single control or control system, and the benefits or savings derived by doing so. Benefits must always exceed costs. Before instituting any new procedures for control, management should first determine that the anticipated savings will be greater than the cost of the new procedures.

IV. KEY TERMS

Following are the key terms discussed in the chapter. It is very important to know these terms and their definitions so you can use them correctly in discussions and in further reading and study. Use the blank spaces to write in definitions.

> Budget

12

Control

Control systems

Control process

Cost control

Cost/benefit ratio

Flexible budget

Operating budget

Procedures

Quality standards

Quantity standards

Sales control

Standards

Standard cost

Standard procedures

Static budget

V. SELF-TEST

<u>MATCHING</u>

	TERMS	DEFINITIONS
_____1	Flexible budget	a. Collection of control techniques and procedures in use in a given food and beverage operation
_____2	Quality standards	b. Processes used to optimize numbers of customers, maximize profits, and to ensure that all sales result in appropriate revenue
_____3	Cost/benefit ratio	c. A budget prepared for more than one level of business activity
_____4	Standard cost	d. A budget prepared for one level of business activity
_____5	Control systems	e. Rules or measures established for making comparisons and judgments about the degree of excellence of raw materials, finished products, or work
_____6	Quantity standards	f. The process used by managers to regulate costs and guard against excessive costs
_____7	Static budget	g. Measures of weight, count, or volume used to make comparisons or judgments
_____8	Standard procedures	h. The relationship between the costs incurred in instituting and maintaining a single control or control system, and the benefits or savings derived by doing so
_____9	Cost control	i. Those procedures that have been established as the correct methods, routines, and techniques for day-to-day operations
_____10	Sales control	j. The cost of goods or services identified and accepted by management

MULTIPLE CHOICE

11. Responsibility for every aspect of any food and beverage operation rests with:
a. the board of directors
b. management
c. steward
d. whoever is responsible for cash handling

12. Food grades are examples of:
a. quality standards
b. quantity standards
c. production records
d. standard costs

13. Eliminating excessive costs for food, beverage, and labor is the ultimate goal of:
a. scheduling personnel
b. disciplining employees
c. training employees
d. cost control

14. Standardized bowls, cups, and ladles are examples of:
a. quality standards
b. quantity standards
c. production records
d. production standards

15. Which cost is both realistic and an ideal simultaneously?
a. Actual cost
b. Standard cost
c. Prime cost
d. Variable cost

16. Which of the following are control techniques?
a. Preparing and following budgets
b. Disciplining employees
c. Establishing procedures
d. All of the above

17. The established methods, routines, and techniques for day-to-day operations are:
a. procedures
b. standard procedures
c. quality standards
d. rules

18. Discipline is:
a. observing and correcting employee actions
b. setting an example
c. used only if corrective action failed
d. termination

19. An operating budget normally is prepared by using:
a. historical data and other financial records
b. records and receipts
c. standard costs and procedures
d. only food figures

20. When preparing an operating budget, which would a restaurant manager consider as an external factor?
a. Economic conditions in the community
b. Plans to increase menu prices
c. Anticipated changes in number of seats
d. An increase in employee wages

ESSAY/PROBLEMS

21. Why won't cost control ensure profitability?

22. Give an example of each of the following control techniques from your work experiences.

A	Establishing standards	
B	Establishing procedures	
C	Training	
D	Setting examples	
E	Observing and correcting employee actions	
F	Requiring records and reports	
G	Disciplining employees	

23. Explain the control process.

24. Discuss the costs and benefits of using a computerized dispensing device for the bar.

16

25. The information below has been prepared by the manager of the Continental Restaurant. It represents his best estimates of sales and various costs for the coming year. Using this information, prepare an operating budget for the coming year. Follow the illustration on page 59 of the main book *Principles of Food, Beverage, and Labor Cost Controls, Ninth Edition.*

Food sales: $380,000
Beverage sales: $80,000
Cost of food: 37% of food sales
Cost of beverages: 25% of beverage sales
Variable salaries and wages: 20% of food sales
Fixed salaries and wages: $40,000
Employee benefit: 24% of total salaries and wages
Other controllable expenses: $55,000
Depreciation: $23,000
Interest: $4,500
Occupancy costs: $33,000

Chapter 3
COST/VOLUME/PROFIT RELATIONSHIPS

I. LEARNING OBJECTIVES

Refer to these learning objectives while you are reading the chapter. They will help you focus in on the important points discussed in the chapter. Think of the learning objectives as questions that you will answer while reading the chapter.

1. State the cost/volume/profit equation and explain the relationships that exist among its components.
2. Define the terms variable rate and contribution rate.
3. Apply the formulas used to determine sales in dollars; sales in units; variable costs; fixed costs; profit; contribution rate; contribution margin; variable rate; and break-even point.

II. CHAPTER OUTLINE

Following are the key headings from this chapter. The purpose of this outline is to help you organize the chapter's main topics. It is also designed to allow you to write key points about each topic in the blank spaces provided. While you are reading the chapter, be sure to take notes using this outline and you will certainly gain a better understanding of the chapter.

1. Introduction

2. The Cost/Volume/Profit Equation

3. Variable Rate and Contribution Rate

        A. Variable Rate

        B. Contribution Rate

4. Break-Even Point

5. Cost/Volume/Profit Calculations for the Graduate Restaurant

6. Contribution Margin

7. Cost Control and the Cost/Volume/Profit Equation

18

III. KEY IDEAS

1. Relationships exist between and among sales, cost of sales, cost of labor, cost of overhead, and profit. These relationships can be expressed as follows.

Sales = Cost of Sales + Cost of Labor = Cost of Overhead + Profit

Because cost of sales is variable, cost of labor includes both fixed and variable elements, and cost of overhead is fixed, one could restate this equation as follows.

Sales = Variable Cost + Fixed Cost + Profit

The key to understanding cost/volume/profit relationships lies in understanding that fixed costs exist in an operation regardless of sales volume and that it is necessary to generate sufficient total volume to cover both fixed and variable costs. Once acceptable levels are determined for costs, they must be controlled if the operation is to be profitable.

2. Average dollar sale may be determined by dividing total dollar sales for a period by the number of customers served. This is also known as the average sale per customer, average cover, or average check.

3. Total variable cost consists of food cost, beverage cost, and the variable portion of labor cost (usually given as a percentage of total payroll expense). Total fixed cost includes all costs other than the variable costs. These are the fixed portion of the labor cost, other controllable expenses, occupancy costs, interest, and depreciation.

4. Variable rate is the ratio of variable cost to dollar sales. It is determined by dividing variable cost by dollar sales and is expressed in decimal form.

$$\text{Variable Rate (VR)} = \frac{\text{Variable Cost}}{\text{Sales}}$$

If the variable rate is .435, it is the same as stating that 43.5 percent of dollar sales is needed by cover the variable costs, or that $.435 of each dollar is required for that purpose.

If 43.5 percent of dollar sales is needed to cover variable costs, then the remainder (56.5 percent) is available for meeting fixed costs and providing profit. This percentage (or ratio, or rate) is known as the contribution rate (CR). The Contribution Rate is determined by subtracting the Variable Rate from 1.

$$CR = 1 - VR$$

Contribution rate is important in another formula as well.

$$\text{Sales} = \frac{\text{Fixed Cost(FC)} + \text{Profit(P)}}{\text{Contribution Rate(CR)}}$$

This formula can be used to determine the level of dollar sales required to earn any profit that one might choose to put into the equation. By keeping profit at 0, you can determine the break-even point for an operation.

5. Each dollar of sales may be divided into two portions: that which must be used to cover variable costs and that which remains to cover fixed costs and to provide profit. The dollar amount remaining after variable costs have been subtracted from the sales dollar is defined as the contribution margin and is abbreviated as CM. Any items sold for which variable cost exceeds sales price results in a negative contribution margin, which is an immediate financial loss to the business.

6. Break-even point (BE) is the point at which the sum of all costs equals sales, such that profit equals zero. No profit-oriented business ever wants to operate at break-even. The ideal restaurant would have high contribution margins, high sales volume, and low fixed costs.

IV. KEY TERMS

Following are the key terms discussed in the chapter. It is very important to know these terms and their definitions so you can use them correctly in discussions and in further reading and study. Use the blank spaces to write in definitions.

Break-even point

Contribution margin

Contribution rate

Cost/volume/profit equation

Variable cost

Variable rate

V. SELF-TEST

MATCHING

	TERM	DEFINITION OR ABBREVIATION
_____ 1.	Break-even point	a. FC
_____ 2.	Contribution margin	b. The ratio of variable cost to dollar sales
_____ 3.	Contribution rate	c. P
_____ 4.	Variable rate	d. The point at which the sum of all costs is equal to sales, such that profit equals zero
_____ 5.	Variable cost	e. The amount resulting from the subtraction of variable cost from sales price
_____ 6.	Fixed cost	f. S
_____ 7.	Profit	g. The percentage of the sales dollar available to cover fixed costs and profit
_____ 8.	Sales	h. VC

MULTIPLE CHOICE

9. For an operation to be profitable, the sum of its cost percents must not exceed:
a. food and beverage cost percent.
b. food, beverage, and labor cost percents.
c. 50 percent.
d. 100 percent.

10. Sales = Variable Cost + Fixed Cost + _____
a. Contribution margin.
b. Controllable cost.
c. Profit.
d. Noncontrollable cost.

11. When profit is 0, the business is said to be operating:
a. on 0 contribution margin.
b. at a low variable rate.
c. on empty.
d. at break-even point.

12. The Contribution Rate is determined by subtracting the Variable Rate from:
a. 1.
b. 2.
c. 100 percent.
d. 150 percent.

13. If 45 percent of dollar sales is needed to cover variable costs, then the remainder (55 percent) is available to meet fixed costs and provide profits. 55 percent is known as the:
a. contribution rate.
b. contribution margin.
c. break-even point.
d. variable rate.

ESSAY/PROBLEMS

14. Given the following information, calculate total dollar sales.

Cost of sales: $46,169
Cost of labor: 54,466
Cost of overhead: 39,156
Loss: 1,257

15. Given the following information, find contribution margin.

Average sales price per unit $12.50
Average variable cost per unit $6.30

16. Given the following information, find variable rate.

a. Sales price per unit $15.50
    Variable cost per unit $6.00

b. Total sales $223,000
    Total variable cost $91,000

17. Given the following information, find contribution rate.

    Sales price per unit $16.50
    Variable cost per unit $7.10

18. Given the following information, find break-even point in dollar sales.

    Variable rate   .42
    Fixed costs $134,500

19. Given the following information, find break-even point in dollar sales.

    Fixed costs $108,000
    Contribution rate   .60

20. Given the following information, find dollar sales.

    Variable rate   .42
    Profit $20,124
    Fixed costs $60,145

21. Given the following information, find profit.

Fixed costs	$43,250
Total sales	$90,000
Variable cost	$37,000

Chapter 4
FOOD PURCHASING AND RECEIVING CONTROL

I. LEARNING OBJECTIVES

Refer to these learning objectives while you are reading the chapter. They will help you focus in on the important points discussed in the chapter. Think of the learning objectives as questions that you will answer while reading the chapter.

1. Outline the purchasing process in the operations of foodservice establishments.
2. List distinguishing characteristics of both perishable and nonperishable foods.
3. Describe how quality standards for food purchases are established.
4. Describe how quantity standards for perishable and nonperishable food purchases are established.
5. List six reasons that standard purchase specifications are important and provide examples of specifications for both a perishable and a nonperishable food item.
6. Describe the process used to determine the quantity of perishable food purchased.
7. Compare and contrast the periodic order method and perpetual inventory method for purchasing nonperishable foods.
8. Determine order quantities using the periodic order method.
9. Determine order quantities using the perpetual inventory method.
10. List the normal sources of supply for restaurant food purchases.
11. Describe the procedures for purchasing perishable and nonperishable foods at the most favorable prices.
12. List and explain the advantages and disadvantages of centralized purchasing.
13. List and explain the advantages and disadvantages of standing orders.
14. Identify the primary purpose of receiving control.
15. List and explain three standards established to govern the receiving process.
16. List and explain the six steps of standard receiving procedure.
17. Describe the duties of a receiving clerk.
18. Outline the essential equipment and supplies needed for proper receiving.
19. List the categories of information contained on an invoice and explain the invoice's function.
20. Explain the purposes of the invoice stamp.
21. List the categories of information contained in the receiving clerk's daily report, and explain the report's function.
22. Explain the difference between directs and stores, and provide examples of each.

II. CHAPTER OUTLINE

Following are the key headings from this chapter. The purpose of this outline is to help you organize the chapter's main topics. It is also designed to allow you to write key points about each topic in the blank spaces provided. While you are reading the chapter, be sure to take notes using this outline and you will certainly gain a better understanding of the chapter.

1. Responsibility for Purchasing

2. Control Process and Purchasing

3. Perishables and Nonperishables

4. Developing Standards and Standard Procedures

5. Establishing Quality Standards

6. Establishing Quantity Standards

    A. Perishables

    B. Nonperishables

        • Periodic Order Method

        • Perpetual Inventory Method

7. Establishing Standards for Prices

    A. Perishables

    B. Nonperishables

8. Centralized Purchasing

    A. Advantages

    B. Disadvantages

9. Standing Orders

10. Receiving Controls

11. Establishing Standards for Receiving

12. The Invoice

13. Establishing Standard Procedures for Receiving

        A. Verifying Quantity, Quality, and Price

        B. Stamping the Invoice

        C. Listing Invoices on Receiving Clerk's Daily Report

        D. Forwarding Completed Paperwork

        E. Moving All Delivered Food

14. Completing the Control Process

III. KEY IDEAS

1. The primary purpose for establishing control over purchasing and receiving control is to ensure a continuing supply of sufficient quantities of the necessary foods, each of the quality appropriate to its intended use, purchased at the most favorable price, and to verify that the quantity, quality, and price of each item delivered conforms to the order placed. Therefore, standards must be developed for:

        1. The quality of foods purchased.
        2. The quantity of food purchased.
        3. The prices at which food is purchased.

2. The types of foods to be purchased for any foodservice enterprise may be divided into two categories: perishables (fresh foods) and nonperishables (staples).

3. It is important that the food controller, in cooperation with other members of the management team, draw up the list of all food items to be purchased, including those specific and distinctive characteristics that best describe the desired quality of each. These carefully written descriptions are known as standard purchase specifications. Once these standard purchase specifications have been written and agreed upon by the management team, they are often duplicated and distributed to potential purveyors to ensure that each fully understands the restaurant's exact requirements.

4. Quantity standards for purchasing are subject to continual review and revision, often on a daily basis. All foods deteriorate in time, some more quickly than others, and it is the job of the food controller to provide a system that will ensure that only those quantities are purchased that will be needed immediately or in the relatively near future. In cooperation with the steward, the food controller does this by instituting procedures for determining the appropriate purchase quantity for each item that should be purchased. These procedures are based principally on the useful life of the commodity.

5. A basic requirement of determining quantities needed of perishables is to take a daily inventory. A very important and useful tool for the steward to use in taking this daily inventory is a standard

form called the "Steward's Market Quotation List." After taking the daily inventory, the next step requires that determinations be made of anticipated total needs for each item, based on future menus and often on experience as well. For each required item, the steward subtracts the amount on hand from the total anticipated need and enters the difference in the "Wanted" column. This difference is the amount that should be ordered to bring supply up to the total quantity required.

6. Perhaps the most common method for maintaining stores' inventories at appropriate levels is the so-called periodic method, which, in contrast to methods for ordering perishables, permits comparatively infrequent ordering. The calculation of the amount of each item to order is as follows.

> Amount required for the upcoming period
> - Amount presently on hand
> + Amount wanted on hand at the end of
>   the period to last until the next delivery
> = Amount to order

When using this method, you must constantly review two quantities used in the formula: normal usage and desired ending inventory. After all, many changes occur in usage from period to period. Bin cards can give you some help.

Using the perpetual inventory method, each item has a perpetual inventory card on which is recorded all purchases and issues. In this manner, it is possible at any given time merely to consult the card to determine how much of an item is in stock at the moment. Additional card information, including the name and address of the supplier and the most recent purchase price for the item, facilitates ordering.

You can make ordering easier yet by recording the reorder point (the number of units to which the supply on hand should decrease before ordering), par stock (the maximum quantity of any items that should be on hand), and reorder quantity (the amount that will be ordered each time the quantity of an item goes down to the reorder point) on the card too. The calculation of reorder would be as follows.

> Par Stock
> - Reorder Point
> = Subtotal
> + Normal usage until delivery
> = Reorder point

While the perpetual inventory method is better for control purposes, it requires much time to implement and is generally found only in foodservices with computerized back office operations.

7. Foodservice operators depend on suppliers who can be divided into the following general categories.

> - Wholesalers

- Local producers
- Manufacturers
- Packers
- Local farmers
- Retailers
- Cooperative associations

8. To ensure that purchases are made at the lowest favorable price, the steward must obtain prices from several competing suppliers for each product that he or she intends to buy. The procedures differ for perishables and nonperishables. Because prices for perishables often fluctuate daily, it is necessary for the steward to call several suppliers to determine current prices each time an order is to be placed. Ideally the steward will obtain prices from at least three suppliers for each item and will select the lowest price, also taking into account delivery time and the reliability of dealers in providing foods that meet specifications.

Procedures involved in obtaining competitive prices for nonperishables are somewhat different from those used for perishables. Stewards often get several extensive price lists from wholesale supply houses and use these to compare prices and make selections.

9. Purchasing personnel must be trained and the training is easier when the kinds of standards and standard procedures are in place. There are many acceptable methods for training employees, including classroom instruction, on-the-job training, simulation exercises, training manuals, and training films.

10. To monitor purchasing performance, controls to be used can include observing and correcting employee actions, requiring records and reports, or telephoning purveyors to be sure that the prices written by the steward were accurate. When necessary, corrective actions will need to be taken.

11. Under a centralized purchasing system, the requirements of individual units are relayed to a central office, which determines total requirements of all units and then purchases that total. Some advantages of this system including purchasing at lower prices (because of the high volume), obtaining the exact specifications, and fewer possibilities for dishonest purchasing. Disadvantages include less buying freedom for the unit to purchase for its own peculiar needs and restraining the individual unit manager's freedom to change a menu.

12. Stewards commonly make arrangements with certain purveyors for the delivery of goods without specific orders. These arrangements are known as standing orders and typically take one of two forms: delivery of a specific quantity of an item each day or replenishing of stock each day up to a certain predetermined number. While these arrangements are convenient, they do present a number of possibilities for both waste and excessive cost to develop.

13. It is necessary to establish standards to govern the receiving process, as follows.

        A. The quantity of any items delivered should be the same as the quantity listed on the Steward's Market Quotation List or the Steward's Staple List, and the same as the quantity listed on the invoice or bill.

29

B. The quality of any item delivered should conform to the specification.

C. The price should be the same as that circled on the Steward's Market Quotation List or Staple List.

14. The standard procedure for checking in deliveries includes the following.

A. Verify that the quantity, quality, and price for each items delivered conforms exactly to the order placed.

B. Sign the invoice or stamp with a rubber invoice stamp to acknowledge delivery quantities, qualities, and prices.

C. List all invoices for foods delivered on a given day on the Receiving Clerk's Daily Report for that day.

D. Forward completed paperwork to proper person.

E. Move food into storage.

15. The receiving clerk is responsible for checking in deliveries according to standard procedures.

16. The receiving clerk needs purchase specifications, equipment for weighing, and office supplies such as forms such as the Receiving Clerk's Daily Report, and a rubber invoice stamp.

17. Every time food is delivered to an establishment, it should be accompanied by some document that lists the items being delivered. For food, the document is normally an invoice, which is another word for a bill. An invoice is usually presented to the receiving clerk in duplicate by the person making the delivery, who will expect the receiving clerk to sign and return the second copy. This serves as an acknowledgment to the purveyor that the establishment has received the products listed on the invoice.

18. It is generally good practice to provide the receiving clerk with an invoice stamp - a rubber stamp to be used on all invoices. This stamp is used for a number of reasons. It provides for:

- Verification of the date on which food was received.
- The signature of the clerk receiving the food who vouches for the accuracy of quantities, qualities, and prices.
- The steward's signature, indicating the steward knows the food has been delivered.
- The food controller's verification of the arithmetical accuracy of the bill.
- Signatory approval of the bill for payment by an authorized individual before a check is drawn.

19. The Receiving Clerk's Daily Report is an important accounting document. It is a record of all foods received, including the quantity and prices. In larger operations, managers divide all food into

at least two different categories: directs and stores.

20. When filling out the Receiving Clerk's Daily Report, items are checked off either as directs (items that are charged to cost immediately such as baked goods and milk) or as stores (items that are charged to cost when issued from inventory).

21. Training receiving personnel is essential if management expects the established standards and standard procedures will be observed.

22. Even though counting, weighing, and transferring data from one form to another are comparatively simple routines, management must never assume that these tasks are necessarily being done and done correctly. Monitoring is required. To monitor receiving employees, managers can check in deliveries after the receiving clerk has done so and compare results.

IV. KEY TERMS

Following are the key terms discussed in the chapter. It is very important to know these terms and their definitions so you can use them correctly in discussions and in further reading and study. Use the blank spaces to write in definitions.

Bin card

Centralized purchasing

Directs

Invoice

Invoice stamp

Nonperishable foods

Par stock

Periodic order method

Perishable foods

Perpetual inventory method

Perpetual inventory card

Purchase journal distribution

Receiving Clerk's Daily Report

Reorder point

Reorder quantity

Standard purchase specifications

Standing orders

Steward's Market Quotation List

Stores

V. SELF-TEST

<u>MATCHING</u>

	TERMS	DEFINITIONS
_____1.	Bin card	a. Maximum quantity of an item that should be on hand at any given time.
_____2.	Centralized purchasing	b. Arrangements in which purveyors make regular delivery of good without specific orders.
_____3.	Par stock	c. A device affixed to a storage shelf used for recording units added to and issued from stock.

32

_____4. Periodic order method

d. The amount of an item that will be reordered when necessary.

_____5. Perpetual inventory method

e. Fresh foods.

_____6. Reorder point

f. A system of purchasing used by chains.

_____7. Reorder quantity

g. Staples.

_____8. Standing orders

h. The number of units to which an inventory should decrease before an order is placed.

_____9. Perishable food

i. A method for determining order quantities for non-perishable foods.

_____10. Nonperishable food

j. A method for ordering based on fixed order dates and variable order quantities.

_____11. Directs

a. Forms used to record data from invoices for goods received on a given day.

_____12. Stores

b. Those foods charged to cost on the day they are received.

_____13. Invoice

e. Those foods added to inventory when received.

_____14. Receiving Clerk's Daily Report

d. A bill from a vendor for goods or services.

MULTIPLE CHOICE

15. Which of the following is a perishable food item?
a. Bottled soft drinks.
b. Canned tomatoes.
c. Oranges.
d. Flour.

16. Which of the following is a nonperishable food item?
a. Plain yogurt.
b. Iceberg lettuce.
c. Bologna
d. Ground cinnamon.

17. The periodic order method is used mostly for:
a. perishables.
b. nonperishables.
c. variables.
d. controllables.

18. When calculating the amount of each item to order, you need to consider:
a. the amount required for the upcoming period.
c. the amount wanted on hand at the end of the period to last until the next delivery.
b. the amount presently on hand.
d. all of the above.

19. A bin card tells you:
a. how much each piece of meat weighs.
c. the balance on hand for that item.
b. how much to order.
d. how many portions have been sold.

20. A description that might be found on a standard purchase specification is:
a. 10 pounds of ground beef.
c. a small bag of ground beef.
b. a box of ground beef.
d. 4-ounce hamburger patties.

21. The maximum quantity of any item that should be on hand at any given time is the:
a. reorder point.
c. par stock.
b. reorder control.
d. perpetual inventory method.

22. Which inventory method is better for control?
a. Periodic method.
c. Par stock method.
b. Perpetual inventory method.
d. Reorder method.

23. Which of the following is a supplier to foodservice operators?
a. Wholesalers.
c. Packers.
b. Manufacturers.
d. All of the above.

24. To ensure that purchases are made at the lowest favorable price, the steward must:
a. use par stocks accurately.
c. obtain prices from several competing suppliers.
b. limit purchasing to wholesalers.
d. order using the periodic method.

25. A copy of the standard purchase specifications is a necessary tool of the receiving clerk so that the:
a. quantity of food items can be checked.
c. quality of food items can be checked.
b. price of food items can be checked.
d. invoices can be verified.

26. The receiving clerk needs to verify quantity, price, and _____ for each item delivered.
a. invoice.
c. specifications.
b. descriptions.
d. quality.

27. Which of the following is an example of directs?
a. Bread.
c. Canned sauce.
b. Jarred preserves.
d. Spices.

28. Which of the following is an example of stores?
a. Fresh fruits.
c. Fresh pies.
b. Cheese.
d. Dry oatmeal.

29. The Receiving Clerk's Daily Report is forwarded to:

a. the manager, food controller, and beverage controller.

b. the receiving clerk, cashier, and the accounting department.

c. the food controller, bookkeeper, and the manager.

d. the steward, the food controller, and the accounting department.

ESSAY/PROBLEMS

30. Yardley Pizzeria uses the periodic order method for ordering pizza sauce weekly. Determine how much they need to order (in cases) today given the following.

- Normal usage is three cases (6 cans/case) per week.
- Quantity on hand is 6 cans.
- Desired ending inventory is 10 cans.

31. The Midtown Coffee Shop uses the perpetual order method. One of the items to be ordered is canned tomato juice. Determine reorder point and reorder quantity given the following.

- Normal usage is 4 cans per day.
- It takes five days to get delivery of tomato juice.
- Par stock is 48 cans.
- Cans come packed 12 to a case.

32. Describe methods for training employees responsible for purchasing foods.

33. Explain the advantages and disadvantages of centralized purchasing.

34. Explain the advantages and disadvantages of standing orders.

35. What is an invoice stamp and why is it used?

36. The receiving clerk at Flamingo's Restaurant also does the purchasing. Name one advantage and one disadvantage of this.

37. Why should hours be set for when deliveries can be made?

Chapter 5
FOOD STORING AND ISSUING CONTROL

I. LEARNING OBJECTIVES

Refer to these learning objectives while you are reading the chapter. They will help you focus in on the important points discussed in the chapter. Think of the learning objectives as questions that you will answer while reading the chapter.

1. List and explain three causes of unplanned costs that can develop while food is in storage.
2. List and explain five principal concerns that can be addressed by implementing standards for storing food.
3. Identify optimum storage temperatures for the five classifications of perishable foods.
4. Explain the importance of establishing standards for each of the following: storage temperatures for foods; storage containers for foods; shelving; cleanliness of storage facilities; and assigned locations for the storage of each particular food.
5. Explain the principle of stock rotation as applied to foodservice.
6. Distinguish between issuing procedures for directs and those for stores.
7. Describe the process used to price and extend a food requisition.
8. Explain the difference between interunit and intraunit transfers, and give two examples of each.
9. Explain the significance of transfers in determining accurate food costs.

II. CHAPTER OUTLINE

Following are the key headings from this chapter. The purpose of this outline is to help you organize the chapter's main topics. It is also designed to allow you to write key points about each topic in the blank spaces provided. While you are reading the chapter, be sure to take notes using this outline and you will certainly gain a better understanding of the chapter.

1. Introduction

2. Storing Control: Establishing Standards and Standard Procedures for Storing

      A. Condition of Facilities and Equipment

- Temperature

- Storage Containers

- Shelving

- Cleanliness

B. Arrangement of Foods

- Fixing Definite Location

- Rotation of Stock

- Availability According to Use

C. Location of Storage Facilities

D. Security

E. Dating and Pricing

3. Issuing Control: Establishing Standards and Standard Procedures for Issuing

A. Physical Movement of Foods from Storage Facilities

B. Record Keeping for Issued Foods

- Stores

- The Requisition

- Pricing the Requisition

- Staples

4. Food and Beverage Transfers

A. Intraunit Transfers

- Between Bar and Kitchen

- Between Kitchen and Kitchen

B. Interunit Transfers

III. KEY IDEAS

1.   Three causes of unplanned costs that can develop while food is in storage are spoilage, waste, or theft.

2. The standards established for storing food should address five principal concerns:

    1. Condition of facilities and equipment.
    2. Arrangement of foods.
    3. Location of facilities.
    4. Security of storage areas.
    5. Dating and pricing of stored foods.

3. The storage temperatures for the five classifications of perishable foods are as follows.

Fresh meats: 34 to 36 degrees F.
Fresh produce: 34 to 36 degrees F.
Fresh dairy products: 34 to 36 degrees F.
Fresh fish: 30 to 34 degrees F.
Frozen foods: -10 to 0 degrees F.

4. The factors involved in maintaining proper condition of facilities and equipment include temperature, storage containers, shelving, and cleanliness. Problems in any or all of these may lead to spoilage and waste.

In addition to maintaining foods at proper temperatures, care must be given to storing them in appropriate containers. Whenever practicable, products purchased in unsealed packages should be transferred to tight, insect-proof containers. In the case of perishables, both raw and cooked, care should be given to storing them in whatever manner will best maintain their original quality.

For perishable foods, shelving should be slatted to permit maximum circulation of air in refrigerated facilities. For nonperishables, solid steel shelving is usually preferred. Food should not be stored on the floor.

Absolute cleanliness is a condition that should be enforced in all food storage facilities at all times.

5. The factors involved in maintaining appropriate internal arrangement of foods include rotating stock, fixing definite locations for each item, and keeping the most-used items readily available. The procedure used to ensure that older quantities of any item are used before any new deliveries is known as the first-in, first-out method of stock rotation (commonly called FIFO).

6. Directs are issued as they are received. Stores are issued when a requisition has been written and given to the appropriate personnel to fill.

7. After stores have been issued, it is the storeroom clerk's responsibility to record the cost of listed items and to extend the requisition. When the receiving clerk notes the price of each item on its container, recording cost becomes easy. Once the values of the various items on the requisition have been extended (meaning the unit value is multiplied by the number of units issued), each requisition is totaled.

8. Many problems can occur in foodservice establishments that fail to train adequately personnel

involved in storing and issuing. Possible problems include:

- Foods could be stored in inappropriate containers or at improper temperatures and quality could deteriorate.
- New deliveries might be stored in front of old, with the old spoiling while the new were being used.
- Pilferage could increase significantly if storage areas were not secured.
- One single item might be stored in several locations, with quantities in one area spoiling because no one knew they were there.

9. The primary technique for monitoring the performance of those who store and issue food is to observe the results of their work. To monitor storing and issuing performance, managers can inspect storage areas, observe how foods are being issued, and check that requisitions are being properly priced and extended.

10. Since the goals of food control include determining food cost as accurately as possible and matching food cost with food sales, it is often necessary to maintain records of the cost of the food transferred from the bar to the kitchen, and from the kitchen to the bar (these are called intraunit transfers). Transfer between the bar and the kitchen occur frequently in foodservice operations of all sizes. Many kitchens use such beverage items as wine and brandy to produce sauces, parfaits, and certain baked items. Bars use oranges, lemons, limes, and heavy cream. As transfers are made, items and amounts are recorded and these records are sent to the food controller. The food controller uses them to adjust food cost figures so they are accurate. Transfers between units (interunit transfers) likewise need to be recorded.

11. Issuing control offers many possibilities for computers. Requisitioning can be done by computer as well as transfers.

IV. KEY TERMS

Following are the key terms discussed in the chapter. It is very important to know these terms and their definitions so you can use them correctly in discussions and in further reading and study. Use the blank spaces to write in definitions.

Extending a requisition

Food and beverage transfers

Interunit transfers

Intraunit transfers

Requisition

Rotation of stock

Unacceptable costs

Unplanned costs

V. SELF-TEST

MATCHING

	TERMS	DEFINITIONS
_____1.	Requisition	a. The storing of goods such that the units received most recently are placed behind those already in storage.
_____2.	Interunit transfers	b. A form prepared by a staff member that lists items and quantities needed and issued from inventory.
_____3.	Intraunit transfers	c. A transfer between units in a chain.
_____4.	Stock rotation	d. Unplanned costs that develop from spoilage, waste, or pilferage.
_____5.	Unacceptable costs	e. A transfer between departments in an operation.

MULTIPLE CHOICE

6. Which foods are best kept refrigerated between 30 and 34 degrees F.?
a. fresh meats.
b. fresh produce.
c. milk.
d. fresh fish.

7. A good storeroom practice is to:
a. store foods on the floor.
b. use the LIFO method to rotate stock.
c. sweep and mop floors daily.
d. leave cans in their original cases.

8. Nonperishable foods should be stored:
a. on solid shelves.
b. on slatted shelves.
c. on the floor.
d. with no air circulation.

9. A written requisition is a form listing:
a. par stock.
b. items needed from Stores.
c. items needed from Directs.
d. items available in inventory.

10. Which of the following is an example of an interunit transfer?
a. Between kitchens of the same restaurant.
b. Between the bar of a restaurant and the kitchen.
c. Between one unit of Burger King and another.
d. Between the walk-in refrigerator and freezer.

ESSAY/PROBLEMS

11. Explain what FIFO means in the foodservice industry.

12. What are the benefits of having storage facilities located between receiving and preparation areas?

13. For which groups of foods and beverages is security the most important?

14. Describe a procedure for requisitioning supplies.

15. Extend and total the following Requisition.

Quantity	Description	Unit Price	Extension
10 lbs.	Flour	$0.20/pound	
5 lbs.	Sugar	$0.35/pound	
2-#10 cans	Spaghetti sauce	$2.65/can	
24-12 oz.	Ketchup	$0.50/12 oz.	
Total			

16. If the kitchen provides the bar with significant amounts of supplies for preparing drinks without writing up any Transfer Memos, how could this impact food cost?

Chapter 6
FOOD PRODUCTION CONTROL I: PORTIONS

I. LEARNING OBJECTIVES

Refer to these learning objectives while you are reading the chapter. They will help you focus in on the important points discussed in the chapter. Think of the learning objectives as questions that you will answer while reading the chapter.

1. Explain the importance of standard portion sizes, standard recipes, and standard portion costs to foodservice operations.
2. Identify four methods for determining standard portion costs, and describe the type of food product for which each is used.
3. Calculate standard portion costs using four different methods.
4. Use cost factors derived from butcher tests and cooking loss tests to calculate portion costs.
5. Use yield factors derived from butcher tests and cooking loss tests to determine correct purchase quantities.
6. List the advantages and disadvantages of using standardized yield figures versus in-house yield tests.

II. CHAPTER OUTLINE

Following are the key headings from this chapter. The purpose of this outline is to help you organize the chapter's main topics. It is also designed to allow you to write key points about each topic in the blank spaces provided. While you are reading the chapter, be sure to take notes using this outline and you will certainly gain a better understanding of the chapter.

1. Introduction

2. Establishing Standards and Standard Procedures

        A. Standard Portion Size

                • Weight

                • Volume

                • Count

        B. Standard Recipes

        C. Standard Portion Cost

D. Calculating Standard Portion Costs

- Formula

- Recipe Detail and Cost Card

- Butcher Test

- Cost Factors

- Cooking Loss Test

E. Using Yield Percentages

III. KEY IDEAS

1. The standards and standard procedures for production control are designed to ensure that all portions of any given item conform to management's plans for that time and that, insofar as possible, each portion of any given item is identical to all other portions of the same item. In order to reach this goal, it is necessary to develop standard portion sizes, standard recipes, and standard portion costs.

Standard portion sizes help reduce customer discontent and animosity between kitchen help and dining room personnel. Standard portion sizes also help eliminate excessive costs.

A standard recipe is the recipe that has been designated the correct one to use in a given establishment. They help to ensure standard quality and quantity produced.

A standard portion cost can be calculated for every item on every menu, provided there is a standard recipe.

2. There are several methods for calculating standard portion costs: formula, recipe detail and cost card, butcher test, and cooking loss test. For many menu items, determining standard portion cost can be determined with the following formula.

Standard Portion Cost = $\dfrac{\text{Purchase Price Per Unit}}{\text{Number of Portions Per Unit}}$

For menu items produced from standard recipes, it is possible to determine the standard cost of one portion by costing out the recipe on a recipe detail and cost card.

For some items, neither the basic formula nor the recipe detail and cost card are useful. For these items, portion costs can't be determined until after some processing has taken place. The processing may be trimming, butchering, and/or cooking, such as in preparing and cooking meats or vegetables. There are two special techniques used to determine standard portion costs for these items: butcher test and cooking loss test. The butcher test is used to determine standard portion

45

costs for those items portioned before cooking, while the cooking loss test is used for those items portioned after cooking.

3.   In the butcher test, a piece of meat is trimmed. The amount of usable meat is turned into a percentage as follows.

Weight of usable meat = Percent usable meat
  Purchased weight

The percent usable meat is also known as a yield percentage or a yield factor. This percentage can be useful when comparing similar cuts of meat supplied by two or more dealers to see who offers better value. To determine the cost per usable pound, you can use the following formula.

Total Value of Usable Meat = Cost per usable pound
  Weight of Usable Meat

If you divide the cost per usable pound by 16, you will now have the cost per usable ounce. The portion cost is calculated by multiplying the portion size in ounces by the cost of each usable ounce.

Portion size x Cost per usable ounce = Portion cost

The primary purpose for the cooking loss test is the same as that for the butcher test: determining standard portion cost. The cost of each usable pound is calculated exactly as in the butcher test, only that the number of usable pounds is weighed after the meat is cooked.

4.   The market prices of meat, fish, and poultry change almost daily. As market prices change, the foodservice operator's usable pound costs and portion costs change as well. Therefore, it is good to have some simple means for calculating both usable pound costs and portion costs, whenever market prices change, without having to complete a new butcher test each time. A cost factor serves this purpose and is calculated in the following manner.

Cost per usable pound = Cost factor per pound
Dealer price per pound

     Portion cost   = Cost factor per portion
Dealer price per pound

These factors are very useful to determine new portion costs when the dealer's price changes.

Cost factor per pound x New dealer price per pound =
  Cost of a usable pound at new dealer price

Cost factor per portion x New dealer price per pound =
  Cost of a portion of same size at new dealer price

You can use the following formula to determine the cost of a portion of any given size at any given market price, provided that one has previously determined a cost factor per pound.

Cost factor per pound x Portion size (expressed as a decimal) x
   Dealer price = Portion cost

5. The yield percentage or yield factor is defined as the percent of a whole purchase unit of meat, poultry, or fish that is available for portioning after any required in-house processing has been completed. This percentage is calculated by dividing the portionable weight by the original weight of the purchase unit before processing. These calculations are included in the butcher test and cooking loss test calculations. On the butcher test, the yield percentage is found in the Ratio to Total Weight column on the line reserved for the usable meat. On the cooking loss test, the yield percentage is found in the Ratio to Total Weight column on the line labeled Salable Weight.

Once determined, yield percentages can be used in a number of quantity calculations. The following formula helps to determine correct purchase quantities.

Quantity = $\dfrac{\text{Number of portions x portion size (as a decimal)}}{\text{Yield Percentage}}$

6. There are a number of levels of knowledge and skill needed in food production, from minimal to extensive knowledge, skill, and experience. The majority of jobs in foodservice each has a definable knowledge and skill quotient inherent in it. An owner or manager must address the question of whether to institute comprehensive training for employees or to restrict hiring to those whose backgrounds include the knowledge, skill, and experience required. Managers tend to prefer selecting knowledgeable, highly skilled personnel for those positions requiring extensive knowledge and skill. On the other hand, managers often prefer to select inexperienced personnel for low-level positions and then train them. Regardless of the level of knowledge and skill that workers bring to their jobs, some amount of training is required for all production workers in foodservice.

7. Production control is another area in which computers can be very useful. They can store recipes and portion sizes, and are useful for completing butcher test and cooking loss test.

IV. KEY TERMS

Following are the key terms discussed in the chapter. It is very important to know these terms and their definitions so you can use them correctly in discussions and in further reading and study. Use the blank spaces to write in definitions.

     Butcher test

     Cooking loss test

     Cost factor per pound

Portion cost factor

Recipe detail and cost card

Standard portion cost

Standard portion size

Standard recipe

Yield

Yield factor (yield percentage)

V. SELF-TEST

MATCHING

	TERMS	DEFINITIONS
_____1.	Butcher test	a. The dollar amount that a standard portion should cost.
_____2.	Cooking loss test	b. The number of portions made by a standard recipe.
_____3.	Cost factor per pound	c. The specific quantity of any menu item that is to be served.
_____4.	Portion cost factor	d. A procedure used to determine standard cost of a product portioned before cooking.
_____5.	Recipe detail and cost card	e. Yield percentage.
_____6.	Standard portion cost	f. A form used to record a standard recipe and pertinent information.
_____7.	Standard portion size	g. The ratio of the cost of a usable pound to the dealer price per pound.

_____8.   Standard recipe   h. A recipe that has been
                                                        designated the correct one to
                                                        use.

_____9.   Yield   i. The ratio of the standard cost
                                                        to the dealer price per pound.

_____10.   Yield factor   j. A procedure used to
                                                        determine the standard cost of a
                                                        product portioned after
                                                        cooking.

MULTIPLE CHOICE

11. For optimum production control, each menu item should have a standard portion size, standard recipe, and:

a. cost factor.   c. standard portion cost.
b. yield factor.   d. standard weight.

12. One benefit of standard portion size is:

a. faster service.   c. shorter preparation time.
b. varied selling prices.   d. reduction of animosity between kitchen help
                                                        and dining room personnel.

13. If bread is $0.95/loaf and each loaf contains 30 slices, how much do 2 slices of bread cost?

a. $0.03   c. $0.05
b. $0.04   d. $0.06

14. Calculating a yield factor is useful for:

a. determining the amount of meat to be   c. eliminating the shrinkage of meat during
purchased in the future.   cooking.
b. reducing the waste of inedible parts of meats.   d. guarding against soaring meat prices.

15. Calculate the yield percentage of a rib roast weighing 9 pounds as purchased if 14 portions, each weighing 5 ounces, are yielded.

a. 47.1 percent.   c. 65.6 percent.
b. 48.6 percent.   d. 150 percent.

16. Standard recipes are used in:

a. hospital kitchens.   c. hotel restaurants.
b. restaurants.   d. all of the above.

17. Complete the equation.

        Cost Factor per pound x _____ x Dealer Price = Portion Cost

a. Yield factor.   c. Portion size.
b. Yield percentage.   d. Cost percentage.

18. What is the decimal equivalent of 9 ounces?
a. 0.52
b. 0.56

c. 1.78
d. 1.98

19. An indirect way to monitor production performance is:
a. to observe the cooks during production.
b. to taste menu items.

c. to ask customers for their opinions.
d. to weigh plated foods.

ESSAY/PROBLEMS

20. How can computers be used in production?

21. Determine the selling price for one portion of a recipe yielding twenty portions when the standard recipe cost and desired cost-to-sales ratio are as indicated below.

Recipe Cost	Cost Percent	Selling Price
$35.65	30%	
$62.35	40%	

22. Records of cooking loss tests done on beef round roasts provide the following factors.

Yield factor: .51
Pound cost factor: 1.96

Determine the number of pounds of uncooked roasts that must be purchased to produce 50 6-ounce servings of pot roast.

23. From the information in #22, determine the cost of the portions if the dealer price per pound is $2.49.

50

24. Given the information below, complete butcher test calculations to determine standard cost of the five-ounce portion, as well as yield factor, portion cost factor, and pound cost factor.

Legs of lamb: 142 pound 4 ounces as purchased @ $3.49/pound

Fat: 29 pounds 8 ounces (value per pound is $0.10)
Bones: 37 pounds 4 ounces (value per pound is $0.40)
Loss in cutting: 1 pound 4 ounces

25. You are going to be cooking a rib roast to produce 6-ounce portions. From the information below, complete cooking loss test calculations to determine yield factor, standard portion cost, portion cost factor, and pound cost factor.

Purchased weight: 39 pounds 4 ounces @ $4.50/pound
Cooked weight: 26 pounds 8 ounces
Salable weight: 21 pounds 12 ounces

Chapter 7
FOOD PRODUCTION CONTROL II: QUANTITIES

I. LEARNING OBJECTIVES

Refer to these learning objectives while you are reading the chapter. They will help you focus in on the important points discussed in the chapter. Think of the learning objectives as questions that you will answer while reading the chapter.

1. Define the standard for controlling production volume and explain its importance.
2. List and describe three standard procedures that enable managers to gain control over production volume.
3. Define sales history and describe two methods for gathering the data from which a sales history is developed.
4. List three basic approaches to arranging data in a sales history.
5. Define popularity index.
6. Use a popularity index to forecast portion sales.
7. Describe the production sheet and calculate needed production for menu items.
8. Describe a void sheet and explain its use.
9. Complete a portion inventory and reconciliation.
10. Describe a procedure used for controlling high-cost, preportioned entrées.

II. CHAPTER OUTLINE

Following are the key headings from this chapter. The purpose of this outline is to help you organize the chapter's main topics. It is also designed to allow you to write key points about each topic in the blank spaces provided. While you are reading the chapter, be sure to take notes using this outline and you will certainly gain a better understanding of the chapter.

1. Introduction

2. Establishing Standards and Standard Procedures

        A. Maintaining Sales History

- Manual Method

- Electronic Method

- Other Information in Sales Histories

- Popularity Index

        B. Forecasting Portion Sales

C. Determining Production Quantities

- The Production Sheet

3. Training for Production

4. Monitoring Quantity Production and Taking Corrective Action

A. Monitoring Accuracy of Forecasting

B. Judging Whether Production Standards Were Followed

- The Void Sheet

- Portion Inventory and Reconciliation

C. Par Stock Control of Preportioned Entrees

III. KEY IDEAS

1. The standard for controlling production volume is to determine and produce the number of portions that is likely to be sold on any given day. It is essential that foodservice establishments know this with some reasonable degree of accuracy so that intelligent plans can be made for purchasing and production. Failure to set up procedures for establishing this can lead to excessive purchasing with its obvious implications for cost.

2. To control production volume it is necessary to establish appropriate standard procedures. These include:

- Maintaining sales history
- Forecasting portion sales
- Determining production quantities.

3. A sales history is a written record of the number of portions of each menu item sold every time that item appeared on the menu. It is a summary of portion sales. Establishments that record customer selections manually are those that use the traditional guest checks. Sales history information can be abstracted from the checks. Electronic terminals have the capacity to maintain cumulative totals of the numbers of portions of menu items sold. There are two methods for inputting portion sales data: by depressing a key marked with the name of the menu item selected or by depressing a two- or three-digit code for each menu item selected in a ten-key numeric keypad.

53

4. Regardless of whether the portion sales records are stored manually or electronically, they are likely to be arranged in one of three ways.

1. By operating period, such as one week, so that all sales records for an entire operating period can be viewed together on one page, card, or screen.
2. By day of the week, so that all sales records for a given day for a period of several weeks can be compared.
3. By entree item, so that the degree of popularity of a given item can be seen over time.

5. Sales history information can be used to determine popularity index, which is defined as the ratio of portion sales for a given menu item to total portion sales for all menu items.

Popularity index = Portion sales for Item A
                    Total portion sales for all menu items

The popularity index can be useful in determining whether to continue offering a certain item on the menu.

6. Forecasting is a process by means of which managers use data and intuition to predict what is likely to occur in the future. It is a principal element in cost control because if sales volume can be predicted accurately, then plans can be made for purchasing appropriate quantities of food to prepare.

A usual first step in forecasting is to predict total anticipated volume: total numbers of customers anticipated for certain days or meals. To arrive at a figure, one refers to the sales history to find the total number of sales recorded on each of a number of comparable dates in the recent past. The next step would be to forecast the anticipated number of sales of each item on the menu. If the sales history shows both portion sales and popularity index, the popularity index is the easier to use for predicting. To forecast portion sales of a given item, one multiplies total forecasted portion sales by popularity index for the given item.

7. Production sheets list menu items and quantities in terms that the chef and staff can use to plan production. Quantity may be stated in portions or total production. The production sheet is best viewed as a tool used by management to control production and eliminate waste.

8. Every restaurant offering steaks, chops, and other similar a la carte entrees has had some experience with portions being rejected by customers and returned from the dining room for one reason or another. There are also many occasions when portions are returned because some member of the staff was not listening or made another similar mistake. These returned portions are excellent examples of excessive cost and should not be ignored.

Whenever a portion is returned, some authorized individual records it on the void sheet, indicating the name of the item, the number of the check on which it appeared, and the reason for its return. These entries can be most revealing to an alert manager or food controller.

9. One useful means of determining how closely the chef has followed quantity production

standards requires the use of a Portion Inventory and Reconciliation form. First, each menu item is listed on the form before kitchen production begins. Next, an inventory is taken of any portions left over from previous meals that may be used again.

If leftovers are to be used, the number of portions on hand is deducted from the quantity scheduled for production, and only the difference is prepared. That number is written in the Portions Prepared column. Additional quantities prepared, if any, are recorded in the next column. At the conclusion of the meal period, an inventory is taken of the portions on hand, with the information being recorded in the column heading Closing Inventory.

For each menu item, the manager adds opening inventory, portions prepared, and additional preparation to determine total available. Closing inventory is subtracted from total available to obtain number of portions consumed.

Having determined the number of portions consumed according to kitchen records, the manager obtains from the cashier (or other source) the record of portion sales prepared for the sales history. These are recorded in the Portions Sold column. The number of portions voided, or returned to the kitchen, is recorded in the Portions Void column and then subtracted from Portions Sold. The result is entered in the Total column.

The next step is to determine the difference, if any, between the kitchen records and the portion sales records.

10. Another useful technique for controlling the preparation of quantities of expensive entree items is to ask the cook who needs steaks, for instance, for broiling, to sign a form acknowledging receipt of a certain number of steaks. This may be referred to as the par stock control of preportioned entrees. The number of portions that the steward issues should be equal to the number of sales forecasted for each item.

At the conclusion of serving hours, the cook will have to return those not used in production.

11. Computers can be helpful in developing records for a sales history, for maintaining sales history, and for forecasting.

IV. KEY TERMS

Following are the key terms discussed in the chapter. It is very important to know these terms and their definitions so you can use them correctly in discussions and in further reading and study. Use the blank spaces to write in definitions.

Par stock control

Popularity index

55

Portion reconciliation

Production sheet

Sales forecast

Sales history

Void sheet

V. SELF-TEST

MATCHING

	TERMS	DEFINITIONS
_____ 1.	Sales history	a. The ratio of the number of portions sold for a given menu item to the total number sold of all menu items.
_____ 2.	Portion reconciliation	b. A record of the number of portions of each menu item sold.
_____ 3.	Sales forecast	c. A procedure in which cooks must sign for high-cost menu items.
_____ 4.	Popularity index	d. An estimate of future sales.
_____ 5.	Par stock control	e. A comparison of portion sales records and production records.

MULTIPLE CHOICE

6. A production sheet reflects a forecast and is used to:

a. set production goals for a chef and staff.

b. establish production procedures.

c. explain production techniques to be used in training.

d. inform production personnel of new recipes.

7. A void sheet is used to record:

a. sales errors made by the cashier.

b. portions returned by customers.

c. food items needed from inventory.

d. food items that are wasted.

56

8. One should include in a sales history any information about conditions and events that have affected sales such as:

a. holidays.

b. special events.

c. weather.

d. all of the above.

9. A usual first step in forecasting is to predict:

a. the number of sales for each item.

b. the weather.

c. number of customers.

d. popularity index.

10. The production sheet lists:

a. what's needed from stores.

b. menu items and quantities to be prepared.

c. portions returned by customers.

d. all of the above.

ESSAY/PROBLEMS

11. Compute the popularity index for the following sales. Round each percentage to the nearest .1%.

Item	Portions Sold	Popularity Index
A	40	
B	24	
C	16	
D	32	
E	29	

12. Using the popularity indexes calculated in Question 11, predict the sales for each item if total sales for all items are expected to be 200.

Item	Popularity Index	Total Forecasted	Sales for Each Item
A		200	
B		200	
C		200	
D		200	
E		200	

13. Using the forecast developed in Question 12, assume that this forecast must be adjusted to indicate 15% more sales. What should the adjusted forecast for each item be?

Item	Sales for each item	+ 15%	Adjusted Forecast
A		1.15	
B		1.15	
C		1.15	
D		1.15	
E		1.15	

14. What are reasons for possible discrepancies between the number of portions consumed and number of portions sold on the Portion Inventory and Reconciliation Sheet?

15. Explain the usefulness of the void sheet and why it is used.

Chapter 8
MONITORING FOODSERVICE OPERATIONS I:
MONTHLY INVENTORY AND MONTHLY FOOD COST

I. LEARNING OBJECTIVES

Refer to these learning objectives while you are reading the chapter. They will help you focus in on the important points discussed in the chapter. Think of the learning objectives as questions that you will answer while reading the chapter.

1. Explain the importance of monitoring a foodservice operation to assess monthly performance.
2. Describe the procedure for taking physical inventory at the end of the month.
3. List and explain five ways to assign unit costs to a food inventory.
4. Calculate cost of food consumed.
5. Explain the effect on cost of each of five acceptable methods of assigning unit costs to a closing inventory.
6. Make adjustments to cost of food consumed in order to determine cost of food sold.
7. Distinguish between the terms opening (or beginning) inventory and closing (or ending) inventory.
8. Explain the relationship between the monthly calculation of cost of food sold and the monthly income statement.
9. Prepare a simple monthly food cost report.
10. Calculate cost of food consumed, cost of food sold, food cost percentage, and food cost per dollar.
11. Explain the possible shortcomings of a system in which judgments about operations are made exclusively on the basis of monthly food cost and food cost percentage.

II. CHAPTER OUTLINE

Following are the key headings from this chapter. The purpose of this outline is to help you organize the chapter's main topics. It is also designed to allow you to write key points about each topic in the blank spaces provided. While you are reading the chapter, be sure to take notes using this outline and you will certainly gain a better understanding of the chapter.

1. Introduction

2. Monthly Inventory

   A. Taking Physical Inventory

   B. Valuing the Physical Inventory

   - Actual Purchase Price Method

- First-In First-Out Method (Latest Prices)

- Weighted Average Purchase Price Method

- Latest Purchase Price Method (Most Recent Price)

- Last-In, First-Out Method (Earliest Prices)

  C. Comparison of Methods

3. Monthly Food Cost Determination

   A. Adjustments to Cost of Food Issued

- Transfers

- Steward Sales

- Gratis to Bars

- Promotion Expense

   B. Determining Cost of Food Consumed

- Cost of Employee Meals

  o Cost of separate issues

  o Prescribed amount per meal per employee

  o Prescribed amount per period

  o Sales value multiplied by cost percent

4. Determining Cost of Food Sold

5. Reports to Management

6. Inventory Turnover

III. KEY IDEAS

1.   In addition to providing management with information indicating the financial results of business operation, monthly accounting procedures (such as taking inventory and determining food cost) also provide information that can be useful for assessing the various control procedures established for the operation.

2. Taking physical inventory requires counting the actual number of units on hand of each item in stock and recording that number in an appropriate place, such as an inventory book.

3. There are five accepted methods for assigning values to units of the products in inventory.

1.) Actual Purchase Price Method. Perhaps the most reasonable unit value to assign to the items would be their actual purchase price. However this can be done only if those prices are marked on the units.

2.) First-In First-Out Method (Latest Prices). This method assumes that stock has been rotated properly during the period and that those remaining on the shelf are those most recently purchased.

3.) Weighted average purchase price method. This method is generally used only in operations that maintain computerized accounting records.

4.) Latest Purchase Price Method (Most Recent Price). This approach is simpler and faster than the others.

5.) Last-In, First-Out Method (Earliest Prices).

4. The cost of food sold for any month is determined by means of the following formula.

Opening inventory
+ Purchases
= Total available
- Closing inventory
= Cost of food

5. When using the above formula to determine the cost of food, there are really a number of adjustments that must be made to that figure because it is really the cost of food issued. This is not necessarily the same as the cost of food consumed. There are many common adjustments.

- Transfers. Intraunit transfers include transfers of alcoholic beverages from the bar to the kitchen, where they will be used in food preparation (referred to as cooking liquor). They also include transfers of directs from the kitchen to the bar, where they will be used in drink preparation (referred to as food to bar or directs). Interunit transfers may also occur.
- Steward sales to employees.
- Gratis hors d'oeuvres to bar.
- Promotion expense (meals for entertainment/business).
- Cost of employee meals (determined by cost of separate issues, prescribed amount per meal per employee, prescribed amount per period, or sales value multiplied by cost percent).

61

If these adjustments are taken into account, the monthly determination of cost of food consumed is determined as follows.

Opening inventory
+ Purchases
= Total available
- Closing inventory
= Cost of food
+ Cooking liquor
+ Transfer from other units
- Steward sales
- Gratis to bar
- Promotion expense
- Cost of employee meals
= Cost of food consumed

6. Opening (or beginning) inventory for any accounting period is the same as closing (or ending) inventory for the previous period.

7. Food cost percent can be determined as follows.

$$\frac{\text{Cost}}{\text{Sales}} = \text{Cost \%}$$

If food cost is 30%, it is the same as stating that food cost in the period was \$.30 per dollar sale. Although figures for food cost percent and food cost per dollar sale may be interesting, they become useful when compared to figures for similar periods in the past.

8.   Once cost of food sold and food cost percent have been calculated, they are normally reported to management. The nature of the report must be determined individually for each establishment or unit in a chain. That will be based on management's need for information as well as the availability of that information. If the food control system is extensive and complex, more detailed information is likely to be available. When it is, management is more likely to be better informed and thus better equipped to make decisions.

9. A simple monthly food cost report for management might look like this.

	July 2008	July 2009
Food Sales	$15,000	$14,000
Net Cost of Food Sold	4,600	4,340
Food Cost Percent	30.7%	31.0%

10. Ideally, the readings used to monitor the progress of a foodservice operation will be both frequent and timely. For large numbers of foodservice managers, monthly food cost and food cost percent are not as frequent or timely as needed. Many foodservice managers prefer to have food cost, food cost percent, and other operating figures calculated much more frequently, such as daily

or weekly.

11. Foodservice managers are responsible for insuring sufficient supplies of appropriate foods are available for use when needed. The stockpiling of quantities greater than needed can lead to any of a number of significant problems, including:

- Excessive food costs due to spoilage of foods stored too long.
- Excessive amounts of cash tied up in inventory.
- Excessive labor costs to receive and store foods.
- Excessive space required for storage.
- Unwarranted opportunities for theft.

12.   One technique commonly used to evaluate the adequacy of a food inventory is to calculate how often that inventory has been used and replenished during an accounting period. This varies from one establishment to another and is influenced by many factors, including the amount of cash available for such purposes, the space available for storage, and the time necessary to receive food once it is ordered. To measure how often a food inventory has been consumed and replenished during an accounting period, foodservice managers calculate a figure known as inventory turnover, or the rate of inventory turnover.

Total inventory = Opening inventory + Closing inventory

$$\text{Average inventory} = \frac{\text{Total inventory}}{2}$$

$$\text{Inventory turnover} = \frac{\text{Food Cost}}{\text{Average Inventory}}$$

13. Computers can be used to assess employee adherence to standard procedures for issuing food, to calculate the value of a closing inventory, and to prepare reports to management.

IV. KEY TERMS

Following are the key terms discussed in the chapter. It is very important to know these terms and their definitions so you can use them correctly in discussions and in further reading and study. Use the blank spaces to write in definitions.

Actual purchase price method

Average inventory

Closing inventory

Cost of employee meals

Cost of food consumed

Cost of food issued

Cost of food sold

First-in, first-out method

Gratis to bar

Interunit transfer

Intraunit transfer

Inventory turnover

Last-in, first-out method

Latest purchase price method

Monthly food cost

Opening inventory

Physical inventory

Steward sales

Total available

Total inventory

Weighted average purchase price method

V. SELF-TEST

MATCHING

	TERMS	DEFINITIONS
_____1.	Opening inventory	a. The sum of opening and closing inventories.
_____2.	Closing inventory	b. Cost of food consumed less cost of employees' meals.
_____3.	Cost of food consumed	c. The ratio of cost of food or beverages sold to average inventory.
_____4.	Cost of food issued	d. The physical inventory at the end of a period.
_____5.	Cost of food sold	e. The cost of food issued plus or minus all adjustments (except employees' meals).
_____6.	Steward sales	f. The dollar value of foods from inventory sold at cost.
_____7.	Gratis to bar	g. The sum of opening inventory and purchases, less the value of closing inventory.
_____8.	Total inventory	h. The dollar value of foods given away without charge at the bar that have been previously added to food cost.
_____9.	Inventory turnover	i. The physical inventory at the beginning of a period.

MULTIPLE CHOICE

10. The physical inventory method requires employees to:

a. add opening to closing inventory.

b. calculate from the bin card the number of stock items on hand.

c. count the number of stock items on hand.

d. check the perpetual inventory records for the number of stock items on hand.

11. A method used for determining the value of a physical inventory that assigns the most recent price paid for units is the:
a. First-In, First-Out.
b. Weighted Average Purchase Price.
c. Actual Purchase Price.
d. Latest Purchase Price.

12. If an inventory shows that a storeroom contains 12 jars of mayonnaise, each with a unit cost of $1.90, what is the total value for that item?
a. $12.00
b. $22.80
c. $41.19
d. $47.88

13. The cost of food sold is determined by adding purchases to the opening inventory, and then subtracting:
a. directs.
b. stores.
c. closing inventory.
d. requisitions.

14. If cost of food sold is $20,000, and sales are $40,000, what is the food cost percent?
a. 0.5%.
b. 5.0%.
c. 50%.
d. 200%.

15. Transfer of directs from kitchen to the bar are referred to as:
a. cooking liquor.
b. interunit transfers.
c. food to bar.
d. cooking wine.

16. Steward sales is:
a. added to cost of food issued.
b. subtracted from cost of food issued.
c. multiplied by cost of food issued.
d. divided by cost of food issued.

17. Promotion expense is:
a. added to cost of food issued.
b. subtracted from cost of food issued.
c. multiplied by cost of food issued.
d. divided by cost of food issued.

18. A monthly food cost report enables management to:
a. document inefficient employees.
b. monitor inventory.
c. provide employee meals at a pre-established cost.
d. make judgments about the effectiveness of current operations.

19. Inventory turnover is calculated by dividing food cost by:
a. total inventory.
b. opening inventory.
c. closing inventory.
d. average inventory.

ESSAY/PROBLEMS

20. Determine cost of food issued for September 20XX given the following.

Opening inventory	Closing inventory	Purchases	Cost of Food Issued
$2,600	$2,400	$6,900	

21. Given the figures below for Apple's Restaurant for December, calculate cost of food issued and cost of food consumed.

Purchases	$12,000
Opening inventory	4,000
Closing inventory	3,850
Cooking liquor	110
Food to bar	174
Gratis to bar	96
Promotion expense	152
Cost of Food Issued	
Cost of Food Consumed	

22. a. Given the following, determine the cost of employees' meals.

Employees were served 86 lunches and 108 dinners in May. Food cost is credited $0.90 per meal for lunch and $1.40 per meal for dinner.

b. Determine the cost of food sold in Question 22 given the cost of employees' meals determined in a.

23. Using the figure for cost of food sold determined in Question 23b, calculate food cost percent and food cost per dollar sale given sales of $25,500.

24. Calculate inventory turnover given the following.

Opening inventory	Closing inventory	Food cost	Inventory turnover
$6,782	7,134	17,264	

68

Chapter 9
MONITORING FOODSERVICE OPERATIONS II: DAILY FOOD COST

I. LEARNING OBJECTIVES

Refer to these learning objectives while you are reading the chapter. They will help you focus in on the important points discussed in the chapter. Think of the learning objectives as questions that you will answer while reading the chapter.

1. Calculate food cost for any one day and for all the days to date in a period.
2. Calculate food cost percentage for any one day and for all the days to date in a period.
3. Prepare a daily report of food sales, food cost, and food cost percentage.
4. Determine book inventory value.
5. Explain the difference between book inventory and actual inventory.
6. Identify various causes for differences between book inventory value and actual inventory value.
7. Explain how computers can be used for generating daily food cost reports.

II. CHAPTER OUTLINE

Following are the key headings from this chapter. The purpose of this outline is to help you organize the chapter's main topics. It is also designed to allow you to write key points about each topic in the blank spaces provided. While you are reading the chapter, be sure to take notes using this outline and you will certainly gain a better understanding of the chapter.

1. Introduction

2. Determining Daily Food Cost

3. Daily Reports

4. Book Versus Actual Inventory Comparison

III. KEY IDEAS

1. It is possible to determine daily food cost for any operation if certain procedures and forms are used. Since all foods can be categorized as either directs or stores in food control, the total costs for these two are the two basic components of the daily food cost. The daily cost of food can be determined in the following way.

   Cost of directs (from the receiving clerk's daily report)
   + Cost of stores (from requisitions and sometimes meat tags)
   + Adjustments that increase daily cost (transfers from bar to kitchen, transfers from other units)
   - Adjustments that decrease daily cost (transfers from the kitchen to the bar, gratis to bar, steward sales, promotion expense)

69

$= $ Cost of food consumed
$- $ Cost of employee meals
$= $ Daily cost of food sold

2.   After determining daily food cost, the next step is to obtain a daily sales figure, usually from accounting records.   When both food cost and food sales figures are known, a daily food cost percent can be determined.   To help overcome the problem of artificially high food cost percent one day and low food cost percent the next, many also calculate food cost percent to date.
Food cost percent to date is defined as the cumulative food cost percent for a period.   To determine it, one divides cost to date by sales to date.

3.   A basic daily report will include daily figures for food cost, food sales, and food cost percent.   In addition, it will include cumulative figures for the period for food cost, food sales, and food cost percent.   When the information is presented in this way, it is easier to monitor operations - to compare operating results for similar periods, to make judgments about the effectiveness of current operations, and to make corrections.

4.   Some foodservice operators determine what the value of the closing inventory should be, based on records indicating purchases and issues.   This is defined as book inventory.   Those who determine a book inventory value normally do so to compare it to the actual inventory value, an important control.   Book inventory value can be determined as follows.

 Opening inventory
$+ $ Purchases (Total stores purchases for the period, as listed on the receiving reports)
$- $ Issues (as listed on requisitions)
$= $ Closing book value of the stores inventory

5.   Depending on the size of an operation and the volume involved, discrepancies of some small percentage between book inventory and physical inventory can often be attributed to acceptable causes and are of no further concern, except that employees should be made aware of any errors made. But when discrepancies are more substantial, management has a responsibility to investigate, identify causes, and take corrective action.

IV. KEY TERMS

Following are the key terms discussed in the chapter. It is very important to know these terms and their definitions so you can use them correctly in discussions and in further reading and study. Use the blank spaces to write in definitions.

Actual inventory value

Book inventory value

Daily food inventory balance

70

Directs

Food cost percent to date

Food cost percent today

Food cost to date

Food cost today

Food cost sales to date

Food sales today

Gratis to bar

Promotion expense

Steward sales

Stores

Transfers from bar to kitchen

Transfer from kitchen to bar

V. SELF-TEST

MATCHING

	TERM	DEFINITION
_____ 1.	Actual inventory value	a. The inventory book value of food at the close of business on a given day.
_____ 2.	Book inventory value	b. The total value of the physical inventory.
_____ 3.	Food cost percent to date	c. The value of an inventory determining by adding opening inventory to purchases and then subtracting issues.
_____ 4.	Food cost today	d. The daily cost of food sold.
_____ 5.	Daily food inventory balance	e. The cumulative ratio of food cost to food sales.

MULTIPLE CHOICE

6. A major advantage of the daily food cost report is that it:
a. is easier to prepare than the monthly food cost report.
b. can be prepared quickly.
c. allows management to make day-to-day operating decisions.
d. reduces excessive costs.

7. The Daily Cost of Food Consumed can be determined by first adding Directs and:
a. Stores.
b. Transfers from the kitchen to the bar.
c. Gratis to bar.
d. Steward sales.

8. Undesirably high food cost percent may be due to:
a. overpurchasing of directs.
b. excessive issuing of foods from stores.
c. theft.
d. all of the above.

9. Closing Book Value of the Stores Inventory can be determined by subtracting Issues from:
a. Total available.
b. Opening inventory.
c. Closing inventory.
d. Purchases.

10. An important element in the control process is to book inventory values with:
a. purchases.
b. issues.
c. actual inventory value.
d. receiving records.

11. Use the information below to determine food cost and food cost percent today and to date for the Thruway Diner.

Date	Directs	Stores	Bar-to Kitchen	Kitchen to Bar	Sales		Food Cost		Food Cost %	
					Today	To Date	Today	To Date	Today	To Date
6/15	$150	$160	0	0	$1,200					
6/16	$185	$175	$15	$10	$1,500					

12. Use the information given below to determine the book value of the stores inventory on the morning of June 4.

Closing Inventory for May: $10.153.88

Date	Purchases	Issues	Balance
June 1	$456.22	$562.58	
June 2	$398.38	$723.34	
June 3	$501.39	$644.39	

13. What is the dollar difference between the book inventory in Question 12 and actual inventory of $9,000.00?

Chapter 10
MONITORING FOODSERVICE OPERATIONS III: ACTUAL VERSUS STANDARD COSTS

I. LEARNING OBJECTIVES

Refer to these learning objectives while you are reading the chapter. They will help you focus in on the important points discussed in the chapter. Think of the learning objectives as questions that you will answer while reading the chapter.

1. Define standard cost and explain how it is calculated.
2. Describe how to use a menu pre-cost and abstract form.
3. List three ways an undesirable forecasted food cost percentage could be changed.
4. Define potential savings and list several conditions that affect it.
5. Distinguish between daily and periodic calculation of standard cost and potential savings.

II. CHAPTER OUTLINE

Following are the key headings from this chapter. The purpose of this outline is to help you organize the chapter's main topics. It is also designed to allow you to write key points about each topic in the blank spaces provided. While you are reading the chapter, be sure to take notes using this outline and you will certainly gain a better understanding of the chapter.

1. Introduction

2. Determining Standard Cost

3. Comparing Actual and Standard Costs

4. Daily Comparison

        A. The Forecast

        B. The Abstract

        C. Potential Savings

5. Periodic Comparison

III. KEY IDEAS

1. Standard cost is the agreed-upon cost of goods or services used to measure other costs. For example, one portion of filet mignon should cost $4.00 in a given restaurant, provided that the staff has followed all standards and standard procedures established for purchasing, receiving, storing, issuing, and producing the item. To the extent that these standards are not followed precisely, the

actual cost of the portion is some amount other than what it should be - an amount that differs from the standard cost.

2. The Menu Pre-Cost and Abstract form (figure 10.2 is helpful in comparing actual to standard costs). The section on the left of the form is based on a sales forecast prepared sometime before a day or meal. The section on the right (the abstract) is completed later, after the day or meal for which the forecast was prepared.

The person preparing the abstract refers to the portion sales figures developed for inclusion in the sales history. These are recorded in the first column, headed Number Sold. The next three columns (Cost, Sales Price, and Food Cost Percent), are copied from the forecast section. To complete the Total Cost column, one multiplies the number of portions sold for each item by the standard portion cost for that item. Next, one adds the column to determine total standard cost of the portions sold. One completes the Total Sales column similarly. A standard cost percentage based on actual portions sold is determined by dividing total standard costs by total sales.

By comparing the cost percent determined on each side of the form one can see how accurate the forecast was. It is useful to develop abstracts of standard costs and sales over a period of some days or weeks and then summarize the results. Taken together, the days or weeks can be considered a test period, with the results offering a good indication of an acceptable level for food cost percent over time.

3. The Menu Pre-Cost and Abstract can be used to project and evaluate the consequences of offering a new or revised menu. There are three means that can be used to change projected costs or sales.

- Sales prices may be changed.
- Standard portion costs may be changed by altering portion standards: sizes, ingredients, recipes, or some combination.
- Menu items may be added or eliminated.

4. Potential savings is the difference between actual costs and standard costs. It may be recorded as dollars, as percentages of sales, or as both.

Reasons for differences between standard and actual costs could include overpurchasing, overproduction, pilferage, spoilage, improper portioning, and failure to follow standard recipes. Reducing potential savings means reducing waste and excessive cost. It will never be possible to completely eliminate discrepancies between actual and standard costs. To the extent that savings can be achieved without incurring other costs, profits will be increased.

5. There are two methods for comparing actual and standard costs. The first requires daily calculation of standard costs and actual costs for the day and for all the days thus far in the operating period - the week or the month. Daily reports are prepared to compare actual and standard costs to date, and the last of these in a given period is a final summary report for the period.

The second method does not require daily calculation, relying instead on periodic determination of standard costs from records of actual portion sales in the period. Choosing one method over the other is a matter for the management of any given operation and should be based on the type of menu in effect, management's need for information, and the availability of personnel to prepare the needed information.

IV. KEY TERMS

Following are the key terms discussed in the chapter. It is very important to know these terms and their definitions so you can use them correctly in discussions and in further reading and study. Use the blank spaces to write in definitions.

Actual cost

Actual cost percent

Forecasted sales

Menu Pre-Cost and Abstract

Potential savings

Standard cost

Standard cost percent

Standard portion cost

Standard procedures

Standards

V. SELF-TEST

	TERMS	DEFINITIONS
_____ 1.	Potential savings	a. A form used to calculate standard costs for forecasted and actual sales.
_____ 2.	Actual cost percent	b. The ratio of standard cost to actual dollar sales for a given period.
_____ 3.	Standard cost percent	c. The cost of goods or services identified, approved, and accepted by management.
_____ 4.	Menu Pre-Cost and Abstract	d. The difference between actual and standard cost.
_____ 5.	Standard cost	e. The ratio of actual cost of sales to total sales for a given period.

MULTIPLE CHOICE

6. To determine the total standard cost of producing a menu item:

a. multiply the portion cost of each item by the forecasted portions.

b. multiply the portion cost of each item by the actual number sold.

c. add the portion cost of each item to the forecasted portions.

d. subtract the portion cost of each item from the forecasted portions.

7. The abstract portion of the Menu Pre-Cost and Abstract form is prepared:

a. before sales have taken place.

b. after sales have taken place.

c. when needed.

d. by receiving personnel.

8. Usually actual cost today and to date are _____ standard cost today and to date.

a. greater than

b. lesser than

c. the same as

d. it varies

9. On the Menu Pre-Cost and Abstract, the abstract side of the form indicates what the cost percent:

a. actually is.

b. should have been.

c. has been running for the past month.

d. should be in order to be profitable.

10. It is best to do calculations of standard costs and potential savings on a:

a. periodic basis.

b. monthly basis.

c. daily basis.

d. as needed.

11. Name five reasons for differences between actual and standard costs.

12. Using these figures, determine actual cost percent, standard cost percent, and potential savings as a dollar figure and as a percentage of sales.

Actual Cost	Standard Cost	Sales	Actual Cost Percentage	Standard Cost Percentage	Potential Savings	
					Dollars	Percentage
$348	$324	$900				

13. Use the following information to prepare a Menu Pre-Cost and Abstract.

FORECAST
FORECAST SALES AND FORECAST COST PERCENT

Menu Item	Number Forecast	Cost	Sales Price	Food Cost Percentage	Total Cost	Total Sales
A	50	$2.45	$6.50			
B	25	$3.50	$9.00			
C	105	$1.90	$4.95			
D	45	$3.25	$7.50			

ABSTRACT
ACTUAL SALES AND STANDARD COST PERCENTAGE

Menu Item	Number Sold	Cost	Sales Price	Food Cost Percentage	Total Cost	Total Sales
A	48	$2.45	$6.50			
B	20	$3.50	$9.00			
C	100	$1.90	$4.95			
D	45	$3.25	$7.50			

Actual Cost: $550.00

Determine:
a. Total actual sales

b. Standard cost

c. Actual cost percent

d. Standard cost percent

e. Potential savings as a dollar value and as a percentage of sales

Chapter 11
MENU ENGINEERING AND ANALYSIS

I. LEARNING OBJECTIVES

Refer to these learning objectives while you are reading the chapter. They will help you focus in on the important points discussed in the chapter. Think of the learning objectives as questions that you will answer while reading the chapter.

1. Complete a menu engineering worksheet and analyze the resulting information.
2. Define the terms star, dog, plowhorse, and puzzle as they relate to menu analysis.
3. Prepare a chart showing stars, dogs, plowhorses, and puzzles.
4. Describe appropriate action to take to stars, dogs, plowhorses, and puzzles when changes are made to the menu.

II. CHAPTER OUTLINE

Following are the key headings from this chapter. The purpose of this outline is to help you organize the chapter's main topics. It is also designed to allow you to write key points about each topic in the blank spaces provided. While you are reading the chapter, be sure to take notes using this outline and you will certainly gain a better understanding of the chapter.

1. Menu Analysis

      A. Column C: Menu Mix Percent

      B. Column F: Item CM

      C. Column L: Menu CM

      D. Box O

      E. Box Q

      F. Column P: CM Category

      G. Column R: MM Category

            • Dogs

            • Plowhorses

            • Puzzles

            • Stars

III. KEY IDEAS

1. Menu analysis provides a means for monitoring the effectiveness of efforts to maximize profits. Menu engineering is a technique used to evaluate a menu by assessing sales volume and contribution margin for each item and thus to evaluate the individual menu items. Menu items can be identified as one of four possible combinations: Star (high contribution margin and high volume), Dog (low contribution margin and low volume), Plowhorse (low contribution margin and high volume), and Puzzle (high contribution margin and low volume).

IV. KEY TERMS

Following are the key terms discussed in the chapter. It is very important to know these terms and their definitions so you can use them correctly in discussions and in further reading and study. Use the blank spaces to write in definitions.

Menu engineering

Menu mix percent

Plowhorse

Puzzle

Star

V. SELF-TEST

<u>MATCHING</u>

	TERMS	DEFINITIONS
_____ 1.	Menu engineering	a. A menu item with high contribution margin and low sales volume.
_____ 2.	Dog	b. A technique used to evaluate a menu by assessing sales volume and contribution margin for each item on a given menu.
_____ 3.	Plow Horse	c. A menu item that has high contribution margin and high sales volume.

_____ 4.   Star   d. A menu item with low contribution margin and high sales volume.

_____ 5.   Puzzle   e. A menu items that should be revised or replaced.

MULTIPLE CHOICE

6. According to menu engineering principles, the items that foodservice operators prefer to sell are:
a. stars.   c. puzzles.
b. plowhorses.   d. dogs.

7. An item that proves to be a dog is one that produces:
a. a high contribution margin and a high volume.   c. a low contribution margin and a high volume.
b. a low contribution margin and a low volume.   d. a high contribution margin and a low volume.

8. Menu items that should be made to increase their contribution margins without decreasing volume are:
a. stars.   c. puzzles.
b. plowhorses.   d. dogs.

9. An item that proves to be a star is one that produces:
a. a high contribution margin and a high volume.   c. a low contribution margin and a high volume.
b. a low contribution margin and a low volume.   d. a high contribution margin and a low volume.

10. The menu engineering catagory that is least desirable is:
a. stars.   c. puzzles.
b. plowhorses.   d. dogs.

Chapter 12
CONTROLLING FOOD SALES

I. LEARNING OBJECTIVES

Refer to these learning objectives while you are reading the chapter. They will help you focus in on the important points discussed in the chapter. Think of the learning objectives as questions that you will answer while reading the chapter.

1. List and explain the three goals of sales control.
2. List and describe eight determinants of customer restaurant selection.
3. Describe the two principal means of maximizing profits.
4. Explain the three most common methods of establishing menu prices.
5. Describe the two principal means of selling products effectively in a restaurant.
6. List and explain the five most important elements of menu preparation.
7. Explain attempts by management to maximize profits by establishing sales techniques for use by the sales force.
8. Explain the importance of revenue control.
9. List and explain the three standards established to achieve the goals of revenue control.
10. List and describe five standard procedures for controlling revenue.

II. CHAPTER OUTLINE

Following are the key headings from this chapter. The purpose of this outline is to help you organize the chapter's main topics. It is also designed to allow you to write key points about each topic in the blank spaces provided. While you are reading the chapter, be sure to take notes using this outline and you will certainly gain a better understanding of the chapter.

1. Introduction

2. The Goals of Sales Control

3. Optimizing Number of Sales

        A. Location

        B. Menu Item Differentiation

        C. Price Acceptability

        D. Décor

        E. Portion Sizes

        F. Product Quality

G. Service Standards

H. Menu Diversity

4. Maximizing Profit

    A. Pricing Products Properly

- Matching Competitors' Prices

- Calculating Prices From Costs and Cost Percents

- Adding Desired Contribution Margins to Portion Costs

    B. Selling Products Effectively

- The Menu

- Layout and Design

- Variety

- Item Arrangement and Location

- Descriptive Language

- Kitchen Personnel and Equipment

- Sales Techniques

5. Controlling Revenue

    A. Establishing Standards and Standard Procedures for Revenue Control

- Documenting Food Sales

- Numbered Checks

- Checking and Verifying Food Sales

- The Dupe System

- Recording Revenues

84

III. KEY IDEAS

1. There are three principal goals of sales control: optimizing number of sales, maximizing profit, and controlling revenue. To optimize the number of sales means to undertake those activities that are likely to increase numbers of sales or customers to a desired level. Maximizing profits requires two essential activities: pricing products properly and selling those products effectively. Revenue control is the process used by managers to ensure that all sales result in appropriate dollar income to the enterprise.

2. To optimize the number of sales, it is important to consider how customers select restaurants. The following are important for most people.

   Location - Customers will normally choose the most convenient restaurant.

   Menu item differentiation - Differentiated goods or services are sufficiently different from others in their class that customers develop preferences for them. A homogeneous product or service is one that is so similar to another that customers do not have a preference and will purchase whichever costs less. There are comparatively few products and services that can truly be labeled homogeneous. Most are differentiated, some more so than others.

   Price acceptability - Restaurant menu items tend to be price sensitive, meaning that there is a relationship between sales price and sales volume. The higher the price of a menu item, the lower the number of customers who will order that item. Customers also tend to choose the restaurant with the lowest prices, given their other choices are exactly alike in every other respect.

   Decor - Each establishment attracts customers who prefer - or at least accept - its decor.

   Product quantity or portion sizes - Portion sizes must be appropriate to the clientele that an operator wishes to attract. Large portions do not always attract the greatest number of customers.
   Product quality - Various segments demand food products of various levels of quality.

   Service standards - Each diner has a personal view, consciously or unconsciously, of the standards of service that he or she considers appropriate for any given occasion when a meal is consumed outside the home.

   Menu diversity - With the exception of those restaurants that offer homogeneous products - such as burgers or pizza, most restaurants find it necessary to have a broad range of items on the menu.

To be successful, a restaurant must meet a sufficient number of these needs to appeal to a large enough market.

3. There are two principal means for maximizing profit: pricing products properly and selling those products effectively. Cost is normally the most significant consideration in establishing the

sales price for any menu item. Another important consideration is the desire to maximize sales. Restaurants with highly differentiated products have more flexibility to raise or lower menu prices than those with homogeneous products.

4. The three basic approaches to setting menu prices include the following.

1.) Matching competitors' prices - Perhaps the most widely used approach to menu pricing is one that might best be described as "follow the leader."

2.) Calculating prices from costs and cost percents - Given portion cost for any menu item, one can calculate a menu price such that the portion cost will be some fixed percentage of that price. If, for example, a restaurateur wanted food cost-to-sales ratio to be 40 percent, he or she could set a menu price for each item merely by dividing .4 into the portion cost and adjusting the resulting answer to some suitable amount to print on a menu.

3.) Adding contribution margins to portion costs - The average contribution margin is added to the portion costs of menu items to determine their menu prices.

5. Essentially a restaurant has two principal means for selling products effectively: the menu and the sales techniques used by the staff.

6. The five most important elements of menu preparation are as follows.

1.) Layout and design - The entire physical menu (the paper, the color, the printing, and so on) should suit the character and style of the restaurant.

2.) Variety - There should be a variety of foods and menu prices.

3.) Item arrangement and location - The items management wants to really sell should be the featured items – the items in greatest supply in the kitchen and with the most favorable cost to sales ratio. Items listed first and at the top of a list are seen first and make the greatest impression.

4.) Descriptive language - The descriptions of foods may increase sales.

5.) Kitchen personnel and equipment - Anyone writing a menu should have a clear, unbiased view of the culinary abilities of present staff.

7. The second means for selling products effectively is to develop appropriate sales techniques to be used by servers, who are, after all, a restaurant's sales force. In many restaurants, managers hold daily meetings with servers just before opening time to review the menu. Another technique is to train servers to suggest menu items or courses to customers that they might not otherwise consider ordering.

8. To control sales or revenue, one must begin by establishing standards and standard procedures that are aimed at one clear goal: to ensure that all food served produces the appropriate revenue for the operation. Without proper revenue control, an establishment may be a financial failure even with excellent cost controls. To achieve effective control over revenue, management must establish standard procedures intended to ensure that food sales are documented (such as on guest checks), priced correctly, and checked and verified daily.

9. To achieve effective control over revenue, management must establish standard procedures

intended to ensure that food sales are documented (such as on guest checks), priced correctly, and checked and verified daily. Numbered guest checks make it possible to assign responsibility for specific checks to particular employees by making employees sign for them. For proper revenue control, sales should always be recorded in a register, and each guest check should be endorsed by the register as the sales is recorded so the check is not reused.

To control revenue, many restaurants use the dupe system. The dupe system is a system for recording customers' orders that provides for two copies of each order, one on a guest check for the customer and the other on a dupe used by the server to place the order in the kitchen. At the end of a serving period, dupes bearing the same numbers as the original checks may be matched against the checks to locate any discrepancies. In most instances, dupes are used only for entree items and certain other high-cost items.

IV. KEY TERMS

Following are the key terms discussed in the chapter. It is very important to know these terms and their definitions so you can use them correctly in discussions and in further reading and study. Use the blank spaces to write in definitions.

Differentiated product

Dupe system

Guest check

Homogeneous product

Price sensitive

Revenue control

Sales control

Sales control sheet

Signature book

87

Signature item

V. SELF-TEST

MATCHING

	TERMS	DEFINITIONS
_____ 1.	Menu engineering	a. A menu item with high contribution margin and low sales volume.
_____ 2.	Menu mix percent	b. A technique used to evaluate a menu by assessing sales volume and contribution margin for each item on a given menu.
_____ 3.	Sales control	c. The ratio of the number of sales of a menu item to the total number of sales of all menu items.
_____ 4.	Revenue control	d. The process used by managers to ensure that all sales result in appropriate dollar income to the business.
_____ 5.	Puzzle	e. The processes used by managers to optimize numbers of customers, maximize profits, and ensure that all sales result in appropriate revenue.

MULTIPLE CHOICE

6. Most food products are:
a. homogeneous.
b. differentiated.
c. signature items.
d. stars.

7. If a menu item is said to be price sensitive, it means that:
a. the higher the price, the fewer people who will order it.
b. the higher the price, the more people who will order it.
c. the lower the price, the fewer people who will order it.
d. the cost of the food to prepare it has great price fluctuations.

8. Most restaurants find it necessary to have on the menu:
a. a broad range of food items.
b. prices targeted at budget-conscious consumers.
c. prices that match local competition.
d. the basics.

9. Which menu description is most likely to sell the item?

a. Teriyaki steak.

b. Scrambled eggs.

c. Ice cream sundae with three scoops of any ice cream, topped with sauce, whipped cream, and your choice of two toppings.

d. Double burger with cheese.

10. The best place on a menu for an item with a low contribution margin is probably:

a. in its own featured spot.

b. at the top of a list.

c. in the middle of a list.

d. on the second page.

11. A simple method of establishing sales control is through the use of:

a. tax records.

b. cost-to-sales ratios.

c. inventories.

d. guest checks.

12. For proper revenue control, sales should always be recorded:

a. by managers.

b. on the Menu Pre-Cost and Abstract.

c. on the Production Sheet.

d. in a register.

13. Using the dupe system, a duplicate copy of the guest check must be given to:

a. the guest.

b. the cashier.

c. kitchen personnel before picking up food.

d. the dining room manager.

14. Dividing a day's dollar sales by the total number of covers results in:

a. the average sale.

b. the standard portion cost.

c. sales per server.

d. the recorded revenue.

15. To achieve effective control over revenue, management must insure that food sales are:

a. as high as possible.

b. a given percent of food cost.

c. documented and priced correctly.

d. profitable.

ESSAY/PROBLEMS

16. Explain the three goals of sales control.

17. What factors do you take into consideration when choosing which restaurant to eat at?

18. If you had to set prices for a new coffee shop in an urban setting, what approaches might you take?

19. Explain the five most important elements of menu preparation.

20. List four fast-food products that are considered to be homogeneous.

Chapter 13
BEVERAGE PURCHASING CONTROL

I. LEARNING OBJECTIVES

Refer to these learning objectives while you are reading the chapter. They will help you focus in on the important points discussed in the chapter. Think of the learning objectives as questions that you will answer while reading the chapter.

1. List and describe the three principal classifications of beverages.
2. Identify two broad classifications of beers and distinguish between them.
3. Identify the three color classifications of wines.
4. Outline the general process followed to brew beer.
5. Describe the fermentation process and explain its significance in the making of alcoholic beverages.
6. Explain the purpose of the distillation process.
7. Explain the difference between call brands and pouring brands.
8. List the primary purposes for establishing beverage purchasing controls.
9. Identify the principal factors one must consider before establishing quality standards for beverages.
10. Identify eight principal factors used to establish quantity standards for beverages.
11. Explain the difference between license states and control states.
12. Identify the two principal methods for determining order quantities and calculate order quantities using both methods.
13. Describe several ways computer programs assist in calculating inventory balances and inventory usage.
14. Describe one standard procedure for processing beverage orders in large hotels and restaurants.

II. CHAPTER OUTLINE

Following are the key headings from this chapter. The purpose of this outline is to help you organize the chapter's main topics. It is also designed to allow you to write key points about each topic in the blank spaces provided. While you are reading the chapter, be sure to take notes using this outline and you will certainly gain a better understanding of the chapter.

1. Control Process and Purchasing

2. Beverages Defined

        A. Alcoholic Beverages

            • Beers

            • Wines

- Varietal

- Brand Name

- Geographic

- Generic

- Sparkling Wines

- Fortified Wines

- Wine Coolers

- Blush Wines

- Spirits

B. Nonalcoholic Beverages

3. Responsibility for Beverage Purchasing

4. The Purposes of Beverage Purchasing Controls

5. Establishing Standards for Beverage Purchasing

    A. Quality Standards

    B. Quantity Standards

    C. Standards for Price

        - License States

        - Control States

6. Establishing Standard Procedures for Beverage Purchasing

    A. Determining Order Quantities

        - Periodic Order Method

        - Perpetual Order Method

    B. Processing Orders

7. Training for Purchasing

8. Monitoring Purchasing Performance and Taking Corrective Action

III. KEY IDEAS

1. All beverages can be divided into two groups: those that contain some measure of alcohol and those that contain no alcohol at all. Nonalcoholic beverages commonly include those normally found listed in restaurant menus under the "beverage" category: coffee, tea, milk, soft drinks, and so on.

2. Beers are beverages produced by the fermentation of malted grain, flavored with hops. Beers may be either lager beers or ales. They differ from one another in taste, alcohol content, body, and processing method. Lager beer is the type most commonly consumed in the United States. Compared to lager beer, ale is typically stronger and has a higher alcohol content. Porter and stout, more popular in Europe than in the United States, are both ales.

3. Wines are beverages normally produced by the fermentation of grapes. Wines are normally classified as red, white, or rose. The color of a wine is determined by the variety of grape used and the manner in which it is processed. Red wines tend to be drier than white wines and range from hearty and full-bodied to light and fruity. By contrast, white wines tend to be lighter-bodied than reds, and range from very dry to very sweet.

4. Fermentation is a natural chemical process by means of which sugars in a liquid are converted to ethyl alcohol and carbon dioxide. Fermentation is used to make beers and wines.

5. Spirits are alcoholic beverages produced by the distillation of a fermented liquid. Distillation is the process by means of which alcohol is removed from a fermented liquid. The fermented liquid may be made from grain, fruit, or any of a number of other food products, including sugar cane and potatoes. The nature of the final product is determined primarily by the basic food ingredient from which the fermented liquid was prepared and the alcoholic content of the distillate.

6. Alcoholic beverages purchased for bars may be divided into two classes according to use: call brands and pouring brands. A call brand is one used only if a specific brand is requested by a customer; a pouring brand is one used whenever a customer does not specify a call brand.

7. The primary purposes of beverage purchasing controls are:

    1. To maintain an appropriate supply of ingredients for producing beverage products.
    2. To ensure that the quality of ingredients purchased are appropriate to intended use.
    3. To ensure that ingredients are purchased at optimum prices.

8. Before establishing quality standards for alcoholic beverages, one must first weigh a number of considerations, including product cost, customer preferences, and product popularity among others.

9. The principal factors used to establish quantity standards for beverage purchasing are:

    1. Frequency with which management chooses to place orders.
    2. Storage space available.
    3. Funds available for inventory purchases.
    4. Delivery schedules set by purveyors.
    5. Minimum order requirements set by purveyors.
    6. Price discounts for volume orders.
    7. Price specials available.
    8. Limited availability of some items.

10. Any discussion of price standards is complicated somewhat by laws that vary from state to state. In general states are either license states (where beverage wholesalers are permitted to sell alcoholic beverages directly to hotels and restaurants) or control states (where the state government actually sells some or all alcoholic beverages through its own network of stores at prices they set).

11. Having established standards for purchasing beverages, the next step is to establish standard procedures to determine order quantities and to process orders. There are two basic methods for determining order quantities: the periodic order method (based on fixed order dates and variable order quantities) and the perpetual order method (uses variable order dates and fixed reorder quantities).

12. To process orders, it is advisable to establish a purchasing routine that requires formal written purchase orders. In a large hotel, the purchasing routine might be the following: a wine steward, as the person in charge of maintaining the beverage inventory and stockroom, would prepare a purchase request in duplicate just after the first of the month. The original would go to the purchasing agent who would write up a purchase order. One copy of the purchase order would go to the receiving clerk so that he or she would know what deliveries to expect and be able to receive them properly.

IV. KEY TERMS
Following are the key terms discussed in the chapter. It is very important to know these terms and their definitions so you can use them correctly in discussions and in further reading and study. Use the blank spaces to write in definitions.

Aging

Beers

Beverage

Blush wines

Brand-name wines

Call brand

Control state

Distillation

Fermentation

Fortified wines

Generic wines

Geographic wines

License state

Liqueur

Mixer

Par stock

Periodic order method

Perpetual order method

Pouring brand

Proof

Reorder point

Reorder quantity

Sparkling wines

Spirits

Varietal wines

Wine coolers

Wines

V. SELF-TEST

<u>MATCHING</u>

	TERMS	**EXAMPLES**
_____1.	Lager beer	a. Champagne.
_____2.	Ale	b. Gin.
_____3.	Varietal wines	c. Miller.
_____4.	Liqueur	d. Lancers Vin Rose.
_____5.	Generic wines	e. Stout.
_____6.	Wine coolers	f. Crème de menthe.
_____7.	Sparkling wines	g. Chardonnay.
_____8.	Brand-name wines	h. A burgundy.
_____9.	Fortified wines	i. Sherry.
_____10.	Spirits	j. Bartle's & James.

11. Which beverage is produced by the fermentation of malted grain flavored with hops?
a. Wine.
b. Beer.
c. Fortified wines.
d. Rum.

12. The process by means of which alcohol is removed from a fermented liquid is called:
a. fermentation.
b. aging.
c. distillation.
d. proof.

13. An alcoholic beverage with a proof of 120 contains how much alcohol?
a. 120 grams.
b. 120 percent.
c. 60 percent.
d. 40 percent.

14. Which of the following is a mixer?
a. rye.
b. vodka.
c. sliced lemon.
d. club soda.

15. For beverage purchasing, standards must be developed for quality, quantity, and:
a. price.
b. issuing.
c. delivery schedules.
d. call brands.

16. States where the state government actually sells some or all alcoholic beverages through its own network of stores are called:
a. license states.
b. control states.
c. brand states.
d. restrictive states.

17. Which method for determining order quantities is based on fixed order dates and variable order quantities?
a. Periodic order method.
b. Perpetual order method.
c. Physical order method.
d. Par stock.

18. The maximum quantity of the item that should be on hand at any given time is the:
a. reorder point.
b. reorder quantity.
c. par stock.
d. current inventory.

19. How can the computer be used in beverage purchasing?
a. To determine call brands and pouring brands.
b. To maintain records of purchases.
c. To do a physical inventory.
d. To monitor sales.

ESSAY/PROBLEMS

20. Describe the difference between call brands and pouring brands.

21. Why do beverage operators establish beverage purchasing controls?

22. Name three factors used to establish quality standards for beverage purchasing and eight factors used to establish quantity standards.

23. Describe the beverage purchasing routine for a large hotel.

24. Using the following information, determine how much of each item to order using the periodic order method.

Item	Par Stock	Usage	Quantity on Hand	Amount to Order
Gin	42	29	6	
Vodka	68	50	12	

25. Given the following information, determine par stock, reorder point, and reorder quantity for each item listed using the perpetual inventory method. Frequency of Ordering: every two weeks
Safety Factor: 50%   Delivery Time: 5 days

Item	Daily usage	Par Stock	Reorder Point	Reorder Quantity
Scotch	3			
Rum	2			

Chapter 14
BEVERAGE RECEIVING, STORING, AND ISSUING CONTROL

I. LEARNING OBJECTIVES

Refer to these learning objectives while you are reading the chapter. They will help you focus in on the important points discussed in the chapter. Think of the learning objectives as questions that you will answer while reading the chapter.

1. Identify the objectives of controls for receiving, storing, and issuing beverages.
2. List and explain the various standards necessary for establishing control over beverage receiving, storing, and issuing.
3. Describe the standard receiving procedure for beverages.
4. List the types of information contained in a beverage receiving report, and explain the report's use.
5. Describe two means for maintaining security in beverage storage facilities.
6. Describe the procedures used to organize beverage storage facilities.
7. Describe the effect of temperature, humidity, light, handling techniques, and storing methods on the shelf life of beverages.
8. List the three types of bars and describe their differences.
9. Define a requisition system and describe its use in beverage control.
10. Compare the techniques for receiving, storing, and issuing beverages used in small restaurants and bars with those used in large hotels and restaurants.

II. CHAPTER OUTLINE

Following are the key headings from this chapter. The purpose of this outline is to help you organize the chapter's main topics. It is also designed to allow you to write key points about each topic in the blank spaces provided. While you are reading the chapter, be sure to take notes using this outline and you will certainly gain a better understanding of the chapter.

1. Introduction

2. Receiving

        A. Establishing Standards

        B. Establishing Standard Procedures

3. Storing

        A. Establishing Standards

        B. Establishing Standard Procedures

        • Procedures to Make Beverage Areas Secure

- Procedures to Organize the Beverage Storage Facility

- Procedures to Maximize Shelf Life of Stored Beverages

- Temperature, Humidity, and Light in the Storage Areas

- Shelving and Handling Bottles and Other Containers

4. Issuing

    A. Establishing Standards

    B. Establishing Standard Procedures

- Establishing Par Stocks for Bars

- Setting Up a Requisition System

5. Training for Receiving, Storing, and Issuing

6. Monitoring Receiving, Storing, and Issuing Performance, and Taking Corrective Action

III. KEY IDEAS

1. The primary goal of receiving control is to ensure that deliveries received conform exactly to orders placed. In practice, this means that beverage deliveries must be compared to beverage orders with respect to quantity, quality, and price.

Storing control is established in beverage operations to achieve three important objectives: to prevent pilferage, to ensure accessibility when needed, and to preserve quality.

Issuing control is established to achieve two objectives: to ensure the timely release of beverages from inventory in the needed quantities and to prevent the misuse of alcoholic beverages between release from inventory and delivery to the bar.

2. The standards established for receiving are quite simple.

- The quantity of an item delivered must equal the quantity ordered.

- The quality of an item delivered must be the same as the quality ordered.

- The price on the invoice for each item delivered should be the same as the price quoted or listed when the order was placed.

100

The following standards are critical to effective storing control.

- To prevent pilferage, it is clearly necessary to make all beverage storage areas secure.
- To ensure accessibility of products when needed, the storage facility must be organized so that each individual brand and product can be found quickly when needed.
- To maintain product quality, each item in the beverage inventory must be stored appropriately, under conditions that will maximize its shelf life.

Management must establish two standards to establish control over issuing: issue quantities must be carefully set and beverages must only be issued to authorized persons.

3. A basic standard procedure for receiving beverages would include the following.

- Maintain an up-to-date file of all beverage orders placed.
- Use the beverage orders to check in deliveries and verify quantities, qualities, and prices.
- Always check deliveries for any broken or leaking containers and any bottles with broken seals or missing labels.
- Note all discrepancies between delivered goods and the invoice on the invoice itself.
- Sign the original invoice to acknowledge receipt of the goods. Retain a copy for internal records.
- Record the invoice on the beverage receiving report.
- Notify the person responsible for storing beverages that a delivery has been received.

4. The beverage receiving report is filled out daily by the individual responsible for receiving beverages. There are any number of variations possible because forms of this nature are developed to the specifications of management in a given operation.

As a rule, beverage receiving reports summarize the invoices for all beverages received on a given day. They include columns for listing quantities received and their values and for dividing purchases into essential categories (wines, beers, spirits, and mixers) for appropriate distribution in purchase journals.

It is generally considered good practice to require not only that the individual receiving the beverages sign the beverage receiving report each day, but also that the individual responsible for storing the beverages sign it.

5. There are two ways to maintain the necessary degree of security in beverage areas. The first is to assign the responsibility for security of the stored items to one person alone. The second way to maintain security is to keep the beverage storage facility locked and to issue a single key to one person who will be held accountable for all beverages in the inventory. The person with the key would be required to open the lock and issue the needed beverages.

6. To ensure accessibility of product when needed, the storage facility must be organized so that

each individual brand and product is stored in the same location. Bin cards help ensure that items will always be found in the same location. Bin cards can be affixed to shelves and serve as shelf labels. When properly used, bin cards include essential information such as type of beverage, brand name, bottle size, and identification number.

The storage area should be kept free of debris that can pile up as the result of emptying cases and stocking shelves. Once opened, cases should be completely emptied.

7. To preserve quality, one must consider the desirable temperature, humidity, and light during storage. Spirits can be stored indefinitely at normal room temperatures (they can even be stored above or below room temperature). Red wines should be stored at about 55 degrees F. White wines and sparkling wines should be kept at slightly lower temperatures. Pasteurized beers are fine at room temperature but unpasteurized beers should be refrigerated.

The degree of moisture (humidity) is of significance only for those beverages purchased in corked bottles, such as wines. They need enough moisture to prevent the cork from drying out (and then letting air into the wine). Bottled wines and beers should be kept away from light. Corked bottles also need to be stored parallel to the floor.

8. There are three kinds of bars: front bars, service bars, and special-purpose bars. Front bars are where bartenders serve the public face to face. Service bars are where customers' orders are given to the bartender by the waitstaff who serve the drinks to the customers. Special-purpose bars are usually set up for one particular event, such as a banquet.

9. A requisition system is a highly structured method for controlling issues. A key element in the system is the requisition form, on which both the names of beverages the quantities of each issued are recorded. No bottles should ever be issued without a written requisition signed by an authorized person, often the head bartender. The head bartenders usually determines the quantities needed at the bar to replenish the par stock.

After the beverages have been issued, the unit value of each beverage is entered on the requisition, and these individual values are extended.

The majority of establishments take the further precaution of requiring that each requisition from a front bar or a service bar be accompanied by empty bottles from the bar, to ensure that the units issued are actually replacing quantities the bartender has used.

10. There may be no training for receiving, storing, and issuing in small restaurants and bars because the owner or manager takes responsibility for these functions. When the size of an establishment increases to the point at which an owner or manager can no longer perform all tasks alone, an employee will have to be assigned and trained to take of these tasks.

A number of national and large regional organizations have departments responsible for developing training programs that include manuals with job descriptions, standard procedures, examples of forms that employees will be expected to use, and other pertinent information. The larger and more complex the organization, the more likely it is that the new employee will be provided with full information about responsibilities and the employer's expectations.

11. One monitoring technique that is all but universal in beverage operations is management's monthly physical inventory of stored beverages and determination of cost of beverages sold. At the same time, management can monitor adherence to standard procedures by verifying quantities received and issued, reviewing the organization of the storage facility, and evaluating the temperature and cleanliness of the storage area and the manner in which the beverages are stored. Managers can also spot-check employees' work, observe employees over closed-circuit television, or verify receiving records before beverages are sent to storage.

IV. KEY TERMS

Following are the key terms discussed in the chapter. It is very important to know these terms and their definitions so you can use them correctly in discussions and in further reading and study. Use the blank spaces to write in definitions.

Beverage receiving report

Beverage requisition

Bin card

Front bar

Full-bottle sales slip

Job description

Par stock for bars

Requisition system

Service bar

Special-purpose bar

103

V. SELF-TEST

<u>MATCHING</u>

	TERMS	DEFINITIONS
_____ 1.	Front bar	a. A card or label affixed to a storage shelf used in inventory management.
_____ 2.	Service bar	b. Bars where bartenders serve the public face to face.
_____ 3.	Special-purpose bar	c. A special beverage requisition form.
_____ 4.	Bin card	d. Bars set up for special events.
_____ 5.	Full-bottle sales slip	e. Bars where customers' orders are given to the bartender by the waitstaff.

<u>MULTIPLE CHOICE</u>

6. In many establishments, a form known as a(n) _____ is filled out daily by the individual responsible for receiving beverages.
a. Requisition.
b. Bin card.
c. Beverage Receiving Report.
d. Banquet Bar Requisition.

7. Security of the beverage storage area should ideally be given to:
a. one person.
b. two people.
c. three people.
d. however many people are needed.

8. Which wine needs to be stored at about 55 degrees F.?
a. Red
b. White
c. Rose
d. Blush

9. The degree of moisture in the air is of significance only for those beverages in:
a. glass bottles.
b. cans.
c. corked bottles.
d. kegs.

10. For control purpose, no bottles should ever be issued without:
a. a written requisition.
b. a written requisition signed by an authorized person.
c. a bin card.
d. empty bottles being turned in.

11. One monitoring technique that is all but universal in organized beverage operations is management's:
a. physical inventory.
b. cost report.
c. perpetual inventory.
d. sales report.

12. Which product should be stored on their sides?
a. Spirits.
c. Beer kegs.
b. Wines.
d. Soft drinks.

13. Establishments that operate more than one bar should:
a. let each bar use the same requisition form.
c. use full-bottle sales slips.
b. prepare separate requisitions for each bar.
d. maintain separate beverage storerooms.

14. To train new employees, which of the following would be helpful?
a. Periodic ordering method.
c. A job description.
b. Perpetual ordering method.
d. Service bar.

ESSAY/PROBLEMS

15. What are the objectives of receiving, storing, and issuing controls?

16. You are in charge of receiving beverages in a posh downtown hotel. Explain what procedures you should be performing.

17. You are in charge of maintaining the security of a beverage storage area. How would you maintain the proper degree of security?

18. You are in charge of a beverage storage area. What would you do to ensure accessibility of product when needed?

19. You are in charge of issuing beverages. Describe how you would use a requisition system.

20. Describe how computers can be used in beverage receiving, storing, and issuing.

Chapter 15
BEVERAGE PRODUCTION CONTROL

I. LEARNING OBJECTIVES

Refer to these learning objectives while you are reading the chapter. They will help you focus in on the important points discussed in the chapter. Think of the learning objectives as questions that you will answer while reading the chapter.

1. Identify the two primary objectives of beverage production control.
2. Describe the standards and standard procedures necessary for establishing control over beverage production.
3. List four devices and means used to standardize quantities of alcoholic beverages used in beverage production.
4. Describe 3 devices associated with computer software used to standardize quantities of alcoholic beverages.
5. Describe the use of standardized glassware in beverage control and the importance of stipulating specific glassware for each drink.
6. Explain the significance of standard drink recipes in beverage control.
7. Calculate the standard cost of any drink, given a standard recipe and the current market prices of ingredients.
8. Calculate the standard cost-to-sales ratio for any drink, given its standard cost and sales price.
9. Determine the standard number of straight shots in bottles of various sizes, given the quantity standard for the straight shot.
10. Explain why bar operations should be monitored frequently.
11. List four techniques for monitoring the performance of bartenders.

II. CHAPTER OUTLINE

Following are the key headings from this chapter. The purpose of this outline is to help you organize the chapter's main topics. It is also designed to allow you to write key points about each topic in the blank spaces provided. While you are reading the chapter, be sure to take notes using this outline and you will certainly gain a better understanding of the chapter.

1. Introduction

2. Objectives of Beverage Production Control

3. Establishing Standards and Standard Procedures for Production

    A. Establishing Quantity Standards and Standard Procedures

        • Devices for Measuring Standard Quantities

        • The Shot Glass

- The Jigger

- The Pourer

- The Automated Dispenser

- Free Pour

- Glassware

B. Establishing Quality Standards and Standard Procedures

- Standard Recipes

C. Establishing Standard Portion Costs

- Straight Drinks

- Mixed Drinks and Cocktails

D. Establishing Standard Sales Prices

4. Training for Production

5. Monitoring Production Performance and Taking Corrective Action

III. KEY IDEAS

1. Control over beverage production is established to achieve two primary objectives: to ensure that all drinks are prepared according to management's specifications and to guard against excessive costs that can develop in the production process.

2. In order to achieve these objectives, management must establish appropriate standards. Standards must be established for the quantities of ingredients used in drink preparation as well as for the proportions of ingredients in a drink. In other words, standard recipes must be established so that bar personnel will know the exact quantity of each ingredient to use in order to produce any given drink. In addition, drink sizes must be standardized.

When standards are set for ingredients, proportions, and drink sizes, customers can have some reasonable assurance that a drink will meet expectations each time it is ordered. Management also establishes a means for controlling costs.

3. Four devices used to standardize quantities of alcoholic beverages are the shot glass, jigger, pourer, and the automated dispenser.

4. In addition to controlling the quantity of liquor used in preparing each drink, it is desirable to

control the overall size of the drinks. Standardizing the glassware used for service makes this comparatively simple. It is management's responsibility to establish the standard portion size for each type of drink and to provide bartenders with specific glassware for each drink.

5. The cost of straight drinks, served with or without mixers, can be determined by dividing the cost of the bottle by the number of ounces it contains to find the cost per ounce. Next, multiply the ounce cost by the standard drink size. If a mixer is used, use the same procedure to determine the cost of the mixer (and add it to the cost of the liquor).

To simply the task of determining standard costs of cocktails and other mixed drinks, many bar managers use Standard Recipe Detail and Cost Card, on which each ingredient is costed out and totaled.

6. Another way to determine the cost of straight drinks is to divide the standard portion size in ounces into the number of ounces in the bottle to find the number of standard drinks contained in each bottle. This number is then divided into the cost of the bottle to find the standard cost of the drink.

For example, the standard portion size for the pouring brand of scotch is 1-1/2 ounces and the bar uses 750 milliliters (or 25.4 ounces) bottles of scotch. By dividing the 1-1/2 ounce standard drink into the 25.4 ounces in the 750 ml. bottle, one determines that each bottle contains 16.9 drinks.

$$\frac{25.4 \text{ ounces}}{1.5 \text{ ounces}} = 16.9 \text{ drinks}$$

7. Perhaps the most important purpose behind the standardization of sales prices is to maintain a planned cost-to-sales ratio for each drink. The drink costing $.90 when prepared according to standard recipe and selling for $4.50 has a cost-to-sales ratio of $.90 to $4.50 - 20%.

8. A suitable first step in training in most operations is to conduct an appropriate orientation to working in the establishment. Actual training would take place at the specific work station. The trainer would explain the standards and standard procedures for producing drinks. This training would be conducted at a time when it would not interfere with normal business and the bartender would be given ample opportunity to ask questions.

9. Bar operations present unique opportunities for employees to deviate from established standards and standard procedures without management becoming aware until well after the fact. For example, a bartender instructed to pour 1-1/4 ounces for a straight shot may instead pour 1-1/2 ounces for many customers for as long as a month (one full accounting period) before management would obtain data revealing that excessive beverage costs had developed.

10. One common approach to monitoring beverage production is to observe bartenders as they proceed with their daily work. Observation could be done by a manager, a designated employee such as a head bartender, individuals unknown to the bartenders, or closed-circuit television.

IV. KEY TERMS

Following are the key terms discussed in the chapter. It is very important to know these terms and their definitions so you can use them correctly in discussions and in further reading and study. Use the blank spaces to write in definitions.

Cocktail

Free pouring

Jigger

Lined shot glass

Mixed drink

Mixer

Pourer

Shot glass

Standard drink cost

Standard drink recipe

Standard selling price

Straight drink

V. SELF-TEST

MATCHING

		TERMS	**DEFINITIONS**
_____ 1.		Straight drink	a. Small glass used for measuring.
_____ 2.		Mixed drink	b. A device that is fitted on top of a bottle that measures a predetermined amount.
_____ 3.		Jigger	c. Double-ended measuring device.
_____ 4.		Shot glass	d. A drink prepared before being poured into the glass.
_____ 5.		Pourer	e. A drink consisting of a spirit and sometimes a mixer, that is prepared in the glass from which it is consumed.

MULTIPLE CHOICE

6. One method of establishing and maintaining control over portion size is through:
a. standard portion cost.
b. free pouring.
c. a pourer.
d. bartender discretion over portion sizes.

7. For straight shots with mixers, the standard drink is controlled by providing the bartender with:
a. a standard recipe book.
b. a photograph of the desired drink.
c. a costed out recipe and the appropriate glass.
d. a measuring device and the appropriate glass.

8. A Standard Recipe Detail and Cost Card would be most appropriate for:
a. straight drinks.
b. mixed drinks and cocktails.
c. wines.
d. all of the above.

9. Calculate the cost per ounce of a 33.8 ounce-bottle of gin that costs $16.90.
a. $0.33.
b. $0.50.
c. $0.66.
d. $0.68.

10. Use the following recipe and the cost of its ingredients to determine the selling price of a melonball. The desired cost-to-sales ratio is 25 percent:

2 oz. melon liqueur	$0.45
1 oz. vodka	$0.18
4 oz. orange juice	$0.03
pineapple wedge	$0.03

a. $2.00.
b. $2.50
c. $2.75.
d. $3.00.

111

11. The purpose behind the standardization of sales prices is to:

a. maintain a planned cost-to-sales ratio for each drink.

c. maintain control.

b. charge customers properly

d. all of the above.

12. Of the following, the best initial step in the training of a bartender is for the manager to:

a. conduct a tour of the facilities, eventually leading to the area in which the bartender will work.

b. quiz the bartender on how to make different drinks.

c. see how accurately he or she does free pouring.

d. allow the bartender to observe another employee in the preparation of drinks.

13. One common approach to monitoring beverage production is to:

a. use closed-circuit television systems.

c. ask customers if they like their drinks.

b. observe bartenders as they do their work.

d. count the par stock in the bar.

14. Computers can be used in beverage production to:

a. maintain standard drink recipe files.

c. print recipes.

b. determine standard costs for drinks.

d. any of the above.

ESSAY/PROBLEMS

15. What are the two primary objectives of beverage production control and how are they implemented?

16. What is the most important reason for having standardized drink prices?

17. What is a common approach to monitoring beverage production?

18. How can computers be used in beverage production?

19. The cost of rum is $.64 per ounce and the cost of cola is $.03 per ounce. Determine the cost of rum and cola in each of the following cases.

   a. The standard recipe is one ounce of rum and six ounces of cola.
   b. The standard recipe is one and one-half ounces of rum and seven ounces of cola.

20. At the Continental Bar, a straight shot of bourbon is one ounce. The purchase price for a one-liter bottle is $17.95.

   a. What is the cost of a straight shot?

   b. If the desired cost-to-sales ratio is 20%, what will be the sales price?

113

Chapter 16
MONITORING BEVERAGE OPERATIONS

I. LEARNING OBJECTIVES

Refer to these learning objectives while you are reading the chapter. They will help you focus in on the important points discussed in the chapter. Think of the learning objectives as questions that you will answer while reading the chapter.

1. Identify the three general approaches to monitoring beverage operations.
2. Calculate value of liquor issued to a bar, bar inventory differential, and cost of liquor consumed.
3. Calculate cost of beverages sold and beverage cost percentage, both daily and monthly.
4. Calculate daily and monthly costs and cost percentages for wines, spirits, and beers separately.
5. Explain how to determine standard beverage cost for a given period.
6. List five possible reasons for differences between actual and standard beverage costs.
7. Calculate potential sales value per bottle for beverages sold by the straight drink.
8. Determine a mixed drink differential and use it to adjust potential sales values.
9. Calculate potential sales values by the average sales value method.
10. Calculate potential sales values by the standard deviation method.
11. Identify the formulas used to calculate beverage inventory turnover and explain how the results of this calculation can be interpreted for maintaining appropriate inventory levels of spirits and beers.
12. Identify two types of computer programs that can be used in monitoring beverage operations.
13. Name the beverage monitoring methods for which computers are most necessary.

II. CHAPTER OUTLINE

Following are the key headings from this chapter. The purpose of this outline is to help you organize the chapter's main topics. It is also designed to allow you to write key points about each topic in the blank spaces provided. While you are reading the chapter, be sure to take notes using this outline and you will certainly gain a better understanding of the chapter.

1. Introduction

2. The Cost Approach

        A. Cost Percent Methods

                • Monthly Calculations

                • Adjustments to Beverage Cost

- Food and Beverage Transfers

- Other Adjustments

- Cost Calculations by Category

- Daily Calculations

- Adjustments to Cost

    B. Standard Cost Method

3. The Liquid Measure Approach

    A. Ounce-Control Method

4. The Sales Value Approach

    A. Actual Sales Record Method

    B. Average Sales Value Method

    C. Standard Deviation Method

5. Inventory Turnover

III. KEY IDEAS

1. There are three general approaches to monitoring beverage operations: the cost approach (comparing cost of beverages sold with actual cost or standard cost), the liquid measure approach (comparing the number of ounces of beverages sold with the number of ounces consumed), and the sales value approach (comparing the potential sales value of beverages consumed with the actual sales revenue recorded). Many operators use just one method.

2. It is useful to compare cost and sales figures on a regular basis to see if the planned cost-to-sales ratio is being maintained. Beverage cost is determined from inventory and purchase figures in the following manner.

    Opening beverage inventory
    <u>+ Beverage purchases this month</u>
    Total available for sale this month
    <u>- Closing inventory this month</u>
    Value of beverages issued to the bar
    <u>+(-) Inventory differential</u>
    =Cost of beverages consumed

115

The inventory differential is the difference between the bar inventory value at the beginning of the month and its value at the end of the month.

3. Beverage cost percent can be calculated as follows.

$$\text{Beverage cost percentage} = \frac{\text{Beverage cost}}{\text{Beverage sales}}$$

Many managers go further in their calculations to get a more accurate picture. They take into account some of all of these adjustments.

Add: Food to bar (directs)
      Storeroom issues
      Mixers

Subtract: Cooking liquor
           Entertainment by managers or business promotion
           Special promotions (such as free drinks)

Some managers also prefer to separate the beverage cost figure into its three components: cost of spirits, cost of wines, and cost of beers. In this manner one can calculate cost-to-sales ratios for these three categories and record them.

4. In some large operations with staff to maintain the necessary records, beverage cost and cost percent are calculated daily. It is not difficult to do: If beverages are issued to the bar daily on the basis of requisitions that accompany the empty bottles, it is rather easy to determine beverage costs daily.

After beverages have been issued, unit costs are written on the requisitions, which are then extended and totaled to determine the cost of the issues for one day. This figure is recorded as the cost of beverages sold on the preceding day. After a beverage sales figure for the day is obtained, beverage cost and sales figures are used to determine a beverage cost percent for the day and recorded. These figures can be adjusted just like the monthly figures.

5. The standard cost method is a better approach to evaluating beverage costs and judging the effectiveness of control procedures. By using this method, management compares actual cost for a period with standard cost for that period. It can be used only by those who have established standard recipes and have calculated standard costs for all drinks. The standard cost method requires very detailed records of drink sales and considerable calculation.

6. The difference between the actual and standard costs represents excessive cost. Some possible causes include breakage, pilferage, and failure to record revenue from sales.

7. The ounce-control method is a method for monitoring bar operations that compares the number of ounces of alcoholic beverages consumed at the bar with the number of ounces sold as recorded on sales records. This method is used today with the help of automated dispensing equipment or

meters attached to bottles to measure the quantities used daily.

8.   Another approach to controlling beverage operations is to determine the sales revenue that should be generated by each full bottle of each of the various liquors issued from the storeroom. Procedures involving potential sales values are generally quite complex and require considerable time and calculation, and are generally only performed in very large operations. Three methods can be used.

The actual sales record method requires that potential sales values be established on the basis of sales of straight shots only and then adjusted daily or periodically by the means of so-called mixed drink differential. If standard recipes are used to prepare drinks and detailed sales records are available, one can calculate the sales value of the ingredients in each type of drink sold.

For example, the preparation of a screwdriver may require one ounce of vodka. Assume that vodka as a straight drink is sold in one-ounce measures for $2.75, and the screwdriver sells for $3.50. The sales value of the vodka is $2.75. The difference, $.75, is known as a mixed drink differential. Each time a screwdriver is sold, sales revenue will be $.75 greater than it would have been if the one ounce of vodka had been sold as a straight shot. Mixed drink differential is defined as the difference between the sales price of a given drink and the sales value of its primary ingredient if sold as a straight shot.

Each day, after sales have been analyzed from guest checks, the number of drinks of each type sold is multiplied by the differential for that drink, and the total bottle sales value for spirits consumed is increased by the total of all positive differentials and decreased by the total of all negative differentials. The net of these figures is the differential for the day, which is typically added to the sales values of empty bottles to obtain an adjusted potential sales value. This adjusted potential sales value should be very close to the actual sales figure recorded in the bar register.

The second method, the average sales value method, requires analyzing sales for a test period for the number of drinks sold of each type. These records serve as the basis for determining the average potential sales value of each bottle.

Assuming that actual drink sales during the test period truly represents the sales mix, a determination of the average sales value for one ounce of gin can be made by dividing 285 ounces sold into $810 total sales. In this case the average sales value for one ounce of gin is $2.84. Because this primary ingredient is purchased and used by the liter, the average sales value of each liter is 33.8 ounces multiplied by the average sales value of each ounce, or $95.99.

Once these calculations have been completed for all primary ingredients consumed during the test period, a chart is prepared showing the average sales value of each bottle used in the bar. Once these average potential sales values have been established, it is comparatively easy to determine the potential sales value of the bottles consumed at the bar each day. One simply multiplies the number of empty bottles of each brand by the potential sales value per bottle. Once determined, this total potential sales figure for the day would be compared to actual sales for the day.

The third method, the standard deviation method, is a modification of the second method and is easier to use. Use of this method requires the establishment of a test period during which management takes all appropriate steps to ensure strict employee adherence to all standards and standard procedures for bar operation. At the conclusion of the test period, the number of bottles consumed is determined from records of inventory, purchases, and issues.

Next, a potential sales value is determined for each type and brand of beverage issued. This potential sales value is based on bottle contents sold as straight drinks. The procedure for determining potential sales value is the same as that explained earlier. If drinks are sold in one-ounce shots for $3.00 per shot, then the sales value of a one-liter bottle containing 33.8 ounces is $101.40. Next, the total number of bottles of each type and brand consumed during the test period is translated into total potential sales values by multiplying the number of bottles by the potential sales value of the bottle. After determining a total for each type and brand, these totals are added to determine a total potential sales value for all bottles consumed during this test period.

The next step is to compare this figure to the actual sales revenue for the test period. Typically, the potential sales figure is greater than actual sales, and the difference between the two is assumed to reflect the sale of cocktails and other mixed drinks as well as the normal spillage. Because the bar operation has been under careful observation throughout the test period, this difference is taken as a standard difference, which can be used in the future for purposes of comparison.

The difference is divided by the potential sales figure to determine, as a percentage, the extent of the deviation from the potential. If, for example, potential sales value were $10,000 and actual sales were $9,500, the $500 difference would be divided by $10,000 to determine that the difference amounted to 5 percent. By reducing the potential sales figure by 5 percent to account for normal spillage and the sale of cocktails and other mixed drinks, it is possible to monitor bar operations in the future, as long as the sales mix remains fairly constant.

9. Most would agree that is important on a regular basis to monitor the size, value, and use of the beverage inventory. The turnover rate for a beverage inventory is calculated by means of the same formulas used for calculating turnover rate for a food inventory.

$$Total\ inventory = Opening\ inventory + Closing\ inventory$$

$$Average\ inventory = \frac{Total\ inventory}{2}$$

$$Inventory\ turnover = \frac{Food\ Cost}{Average\ Inventory}$$

Generally accepted monthly turnover rates for spirits and beers are: spirits 1.5, beers 2.0 (they are more perishable).

10. Database computer programs can maintain perpetual inventories of beverages. Assuming timely and accurate data entry for purchases and issues during a period, a printout of the perpetual inventory could be obtained to compare to the monthly physical inventory. Differences would show the extent of deviations from standard control procedures.

Spreadsheet programs are helpful in valuing the monthly physical inventory and for calculating daily cost percents. Once the spreadsheet is set up, one merely records figures daily for issues, adjustments, and sales. The next logical step, printing a daily report for management is easy.

The standard cost methods for monitoring beverage operations would be particularly difficult to use if one did not have a computer-based file of standard drink recipes and their costs, along with detailed records of sales showing the number of drinks of each type, sold daily and for the period.

IV. KEY TERMS

Following are the key terms discussed in the chapter. It is very important to know these terms and their definitions so you can use them correctly in discussions and in further reading and study. Use the blank spaces to write in definitions.

Actual beverage cost

Actual sales record method

Average inventory

Average potential sales value

Average sales value method

Beverage cost percent

Food and beverage transfers

Inventory differential

Inventory turnover

Inventory turnover method

Mixed drink differential

Ounce-control method

Potential sales value

Primary ingredient

Standard cost method

Standard deviation method

V. SELF-TEST

<u>MATCHING #1</u>

	TERMS	DEFINITIONS
_____ 1.	Inventory differential	a. Ratio of beverage cost to beverage sales
_____ 2.	Mixed drink differential	b. The difference between start-of-month and end-of-month value of bar inventory.
_____ 3.	Potential sales value	c. Calculated sales value of a bottle of liquor.
_____ 4.	Average potential sales value	d. Dollar sales value of a given quantity of alcoholic beverage.
_____ 5.	Beverage cost percent	e. An adjustment to the potential sales value of a bottle of liquor.

<u>MATCHING #2</u>

	TERMS	DEFINITIONS
_____ 6.	Actual sales record method	a. Calculates the potential sales value of all bottles of liquor consumed based on number of empty bottles multiplied by average potential sales value of each bottle
_____ 7.	Average sales value method	b. Compares the number of ounces of alcoholic beverage consumed at the bar with the number of ounces sold.

120

_____ 8.	Inventory turnover method	c. Translates quantities of alcoholic beverages consumed into potential sales values.
_____ 9.	Ounce-control method	d. Compares calculated standard product costs with actual costs.
_____ 10.	Standard cost method	e. Monitors the size of a beverage inventory.

MULTIPLE CHOICE

11. Opening beverage inventory + Beverage purchases this month =
a. Value of beverages issued to the bar.
b. Bar inventory differential.
c. Total available for sale this month.
d. Cost of beverages consumed.

12. The bar inventory differential is calculated by:
a. adding the bar inventory value at the beginning of the month to the value at the end of the month.
b. subtracting the bar inventory value at the beginning of the month from the value at the end of the month.
c. subtracting the bar inventory value at the end of the month from the value at the beginning of the month.
d. none of the above.

13. Once the beverage cost percent for a period has been calculated, it may be compared to:
a. food cost percent.
b. beverage cost percents for other similar periods.
c. bar differential.
d. gross profit.

14. To calculate beverage cost and cost percent daily requires:
a. no more staff than if you do these calculations monthly.
b. food cost percents.
c. adjusting for overhead.
d. more staff to maintain the necessary records.

15. The difference between actual cost and standard cost may be due to:
a. breakage.
b. pilferage.
c. failure to record revenue from sales.
d. all of the above.

ESSAY/PROBLEMS

16. a. Using the information below, determine beverage cost at the Continental Bar.

Storeroom Opening Inventory: $6,487
Storeroom Purchases: $9,644
Storeroom Closing Inventory: $6,689

Bar Opening Inventory: $1,233
Bar Closing Inventory: $1,023

b. If the sales at the Continental Bar are $22,849, what is the beverage cost percent using the costs determined in #16?

c. What is the inventory turnover rate?

17. Using the information from #16 and the adjustments below to calculate adjusted cost of beverages sold following the format provided in Figure 17.1. Then recalculate beverage cost percent based on adjusted cost.

Mixers $455
Food to bar $267
Cooking liquor $95
Special promotions $78

18. What is the potential sales value of scotch issued assuming that:

    One-ounce shots were poured.
    750-milliliter bottles were issued.
    The sales price for all straight shots was $2.50.
    There were 4 bottles issued.

19. Compute the deviation from potential sales given that the actual sales for the test period is $10,000 and the potential sales based on straight shots are $10,300. What should actual sales be if the potential sales based on straight shots were $8,000?

Chapter 17
BEVERAGE SALES CONTROL

I. LEARNING OBJECTIVES

Refer to these learning objectives while you are reading the chapter. They will help you focus in on the important points discussed in the chapter. Think of the learning objectives as questions that you will answer while reading the chapter.

1. List and explain the three goals of beverage sales control.
2. Identify five explanations given by customers for patronizing establishments that serve drinks.
3. Describe the specific steps that bar managers can take to attract particular market segments.
4. Describe two methods that can be used to maximize profits in beverage operations.
5. Identify two important factors normally taken into account when establishing beverage sales prices.
6. Name ten work practices considered unacceptable at bars because they inhibit the ability of bar managers to institute effective revenue control.
7. Describe the essential features of a precheck system.

II. CHAPTER OUTLINE

Following are the key headings from this chapter. The purpose of this outline is to help you organize the chapter's main topics. It is also designed to allow you to write key points about each topic in the blank spaces provided. While you are reading the chapter, be sure to take notes using this outline and you will certainly gain a better understanding of the chapter.

1. Introduction

2. The Objectives of Beverage Sales Control

3. Optimizing the Number of Beverage Sales

        A. To Socialize

        B. To Conduct Business

        C. To Eat

        D. To Seek Entertainment

        E. To Waste Time

4. Maximizing Profits

A. Establishing Drink Prices

B. Influencing Customer Selections

5. Controlling Revenue

A. Bars Without Guest Checks

B. Bars Using Guest Checks

- Pre-Check System

- Automated Systems

III. KEY IDEAS

1. The objectives for beverage sales control are optimizing the number of sale, maximizing profit, and controlling revenue. While these objectives give the initial appearance of being identical to those of food sales control, there are special considerations in bar operations - some legal, some ethical and moral - that lead to significant differences.

2. People patronize bars and restaurants with bars for the following reasons: to socialize, to conduct business, to eat, to seek entertainment, and to waste time.

3. The owner or manager of a beverage operation must determine which market segment or segments he or she intends to attract, and then decide what this segment desires in terms of brands and types of drinks, portion sizes, and so on.

4. In beverage operations, profit maximization is accomplished by establishing drink prices that will maximize gross profit and by influencing customers' selections through promotion of special drinks or menu pictures. Profit maximization is not accomplished by getting customers to buy more. Many states have passed dram shop laws and laws that eliminate the use of the term "happy hour" and two-for-one drink promotions.

5. Unlike food sales prices, the costs of ingredients and labor are not the primary determinants of drink prices. Beverage ingredient costs and labor costs per dollar sale are both significantly lower than those for food, so they are not as important in establishing sales prices. Other considerations are of greater importance in establishing drink prices. These include overhead costs (occupancy, insurance, licenses, and entertainment, to name a few) and significant market considerations.

6. Revenue control consists of those activities established to ensure that each sale to a customer results in appropriate revenue to the operation. In many bars the bartender is responsible for all the work, from taking orders to collecting cash. This dependence on one person tends to minimize the possibilities for instituting and maintaining control. One common means for determining whether or not operational problems exist is to assess the work habits of the bartender, and make sure he or she is NOT:

124

- working with cash drawer open,
- under-ringing sales,
- overcharging customers,
- undercharging customers,
- overpouring, and underpouring,
- diluting bottle contents,
- bringing own bottle into the bar,
- charging for drinks not served, or
- drinking on the job.

7.   In order to reduce the number of revenue control problems to a minimum, management must establish standards and standard procedures for bar operation. Effective revenue control requires that employees adhere strictly to these standards and standard procedures and that the performance of bartenders be monitored by management. Some bars use guest checks to approach revenue control. Other bars do not. Numbered guest checks do give some degree of control.

8.   Using the pre-check system, there are registers available that enable bartenders to record sales as drinks are served and to accumulate the sales to any one customer on one check. The use of such a register makes it feasible to require that a guest check be placed in front of each customer at the bar. When the customer is ready to leave, the check is inserted into the register or terminal and the total sales to the customer are recorded as cash or charge, depending on how the customer settles the check. A the end of the day's operation, the total drink sales recorded in the terminal, plus taxes, should equal the total of cash and charge sales.

9.   An automated bar is both an electronic sales terminal and a computerized dispensing device for beverages. The dispensing device is controlled by the sales terminal. When a customer orders a drink, the bartender places the proper glassware under the dispensing device, inserts a guest check in the terminal or in a separate printer controlled by the terminal, and depresses the terminal key with the name of the drink on it.

There are some significant advantages to automated systems over traditional methods of preparing drinks. The proportions of ingredients are exactly the same each time a given drink is prepared, and the drinks are thus of uniform quality, prepared according to the standard recipes programmed; the quantity of each ingredient is measured exactly, and the sizes of all drinks of any given type are uniform. However, it must be noted that these systems only reduce the possibilities for the development of excessive costs through pilferage, spillage, and various bartender errors. The possibilities for charging incorrect prices are greatly reduced.

There are also some important disadvantages to these systems. Most cannot accommodate customers' requests for drinks made according to recipes other than the standard recipes programmed. At front bars, many customers have negative reactions to automated bars. For these customers, having drinks prepared by a machine takes something away from their experience. In addition, traditional methods of drink preparation often give customers the impression that the bartender is giving them more than the standard measure, a dividend, so to speak.

IV. KEY TERMS

Following are the key terms discussed in the chapter. It is very important to know these terms and their definitions so you can use them correctly in discussions and in further reading and study. Use the blank spaces to write in definitions.

Beverage sales control

Beverage profit maximization

Dram shop laws

Market segment

Pre-check system

Automated bar

V. SELF-TEST

MATCHING

	TERMS	DEFINITIONS
_____ 1.	Beverage sales control	a. Processes used by managers to optimize the number of sales, maximize profits on sales, and ensure that all sales result in the appropriate revenue.
_____ 2.	Dram shop laws	b. A computerized device for dispensing beverages and registering sales at the same time.

_____ 3.	Market segment	c. State statues that explain liability if a bar serves alcohol to intoxicated customers.
_____ 4.	Pre-check system	d. A method for controlling revenue.
_____ 5.	Automated bar	e. Subgroup of potential patrons with similar characteristics.

MULTIPLE CHOICE

6. Overhead costs for a beverage operation typically account for a:
a. small percentage of total costs.
b. large percentage of total costs.
c. 0 to 5% of total costs.
d. 5 to 10% of total costs.

7. A bartender who overpours for some customers is most likely to:
a. work with the cash drawer open.
b. overcharge customers.
c. underpour for other customers.
d. drink on the job.

8. When the visual monitoring of bartenders is impossible or impractical, some degree of control is made possible by the use of:
a. numbered guest checks.
b. automated systems.
c. pre-check system.
d. all of the above.

9. Automated systems are more often used at:
a. front bars.
b. service bars.
c. special-purpose bars.
d. all of the above.

10. Which of the following is priced higher?
a. Call brands.
b. Pouring brands.
c. Generic brands.
d. It varies.

ESSAY/PROBLEMS

11. Why do people patronize some of the popular bars in your area?

12. You are the manager of the Shamrock Inn. What can you do to maximize profit and at the same time make sure your customers do not engage in drunken driving?

13. List 10 poor bartender work habits.

14. Explain how the pre-check system works.

15. Explain how automated bars work and their advantages and disadvantages.

Chapter 18
LABOR COST CONSIDERATIONS

I. LEARNING OBJECTIVES

Refer to these learning objectives while you are reading the chapter. They will help you focus in on the important points discussed in the chapter. Think of the learning objectives as questions that you will answer while reading the chapter.

1. Define employee compensation and list the principal types of compensation common in food and beverage operations.
2. Explain the difference between direct and indirect compensation.
3. Explain why each of the following is a determinant of labor cost or labor cost percentage: labor turnover rate; training; labor legislation; labor contracts; use of part-time staff; outsourcing; sales volume; location; equipment; layout; preparation; service; menu; hours of operation; weather; and competent management.
4. Explain why labor costs and labor cost percentages vary from one establishment to another.
5. Explain why the minimizing of dollar wages is not the same as labor cost control.
6. Define labor cost control.

II. CHAPTER OUTLINE

Following are the key headings from this chapter. The purpose of this outline is to help you organize the chapter's main topics. It is also designed to allow you to write key points about each topic in the blank spaces provided. While you are reading the chapter, be sure to take notes using this outline and you will certainly gain a better understanding of the chapter.

1. Introduction

2. Employee Compensation

      A. Current Compensation

          • Direct Compensation

          • Indirect Compensation

      B. Deferred Compensation

3. Determinants of Total Labor Costs and Labor Cost Percents

      A. Labor Turnover Rate

B. Training

C. Labor Legislation

D. Labor Contracts

E. Use of Part-Time Staff

F. Use of Outside Services

G. Sales Volume

H. Location

I. Equipment

J. Layout

K. Preparation

L. Service

M. Menu

N. Hours of Operation

O. Weather

P. Competent Management

Q. Conclusion

4. Labor Cost Control

A. Labor Cost Control Defined

B. The Purpose of Labor Cost Control

C. Control Process

III. KEY IDEAS

1. Compensation refers to all forms of pay and other rewards going to employees as a result of their employment. In the hospitality industry, employees receive two forms of current compensation: direct and indirect, as well as deferred compensation.

2. Direct compensation includes salaries, wages, tips, bonuses, and commissions. The term salary is used to refer to a fixed dollar amount of compensation paid on a weekly, monthly, or annual basis, regardless of the actual number of hours worked. Wages, by contrast, always take the actual number of hours worked into account. The hours worked are multiplied by the employee's hourly wage.

Tips, also known as gratuities, while not paid from an employer's funds, are also compensation in the eyes of the law and are so treated by federal and state agencies for purposes of calculating such taxes as income tax, social security tax, and Medicare tax. Many workers in the hospitality industry earn more from tips than from wages. Bonus is a term that refers to dollar amounts over and above an employee's wages or salary given as a reward for some type of job performance. Commissions are dollar amounts calculated as percentages of sales. Travel agents and some banquet managers commonly earn commissions on their sales.

Indirect compensation may include paid vacations (the most common), health benefits, life insurance, free meals, free living accommodations, use of recreational facilities operated by the employer, discounts on accommodations at other properties within a chain, and many other possibilities.

Deferred compensation is defined as compensation received by an employee after the conclusion of his or her period of employment. Two of the most important forms of deferred compensation are pension benefits and Social Security.

3. The cost of labor is affected by a number of important considerations. The determinants discussed below are those that have a direct effect on the total cost of labor or on the cost of labor expressed as a percentage of sales. Some affect both.

- Labor turnover rate (a ratio relating the number of departing employees to the total number of employees on the staff and usually expressed as a percentage). The labor turnover rate has traditionally been high (around 100 percent per year) in the foodservice industry. High turnover rates generally result in higher labor costs due to the cost of recruiting, hiring, and training new employees.
- Training. Training can be a key factor in reducing the labor turnover rate in a restaurant.
- Labor legislation. Labor legislation differs considerably from state to state but all states provide for minimum wages and overtime pay. As a labor-intensive industry, the foodservice industry has traditionally employed a large number of unskilled persons, many of whom receive the minimum wage. As state legislatures have steadily increased minimum wages, labor cost in the restaurant industry has been significantly affected. Federal and state legislation also mandates other costs that affect total labor cost. These include old age survivors' insurance (social security), Medicare/Medicaid insurance, workers' compensation, and unemployment insurance.
- Labor contracts. Where employees are organized and labor contracts exist, wages are likely to be higher than they would be in the absence of a union. In addition,

fringe benefits are more likely to be found.

- **Use of part-time staff.** In the foodservice industry today, a large number of managers are hiring growing numbers of part-time employees to keep labor costs lower than they would be if all work was done by full-time personnel.
- **Use of outside services.** Many establishments are finding it less costly to rely on outside contractors for various goods and services (such as frozen portioned entrees or nighttime cleaning).
- **Sales volume.** For a restaurant of any given size, increases in sales volume will result in increased productivity per employee up to his or her maximum capacity to perform. Large restaurants are often able to take advantage of the economies of large-scale production.
- **Location.** Labor costs vary from one part of the country to another.
- **Equipment.** Lower labor costs can often result from doing tasks such as washing dishes with modern equipment.
- **Layout.** Labor costs are higher when the layout of the work areas impedes employees' ability to perform their tasks.
- **Preparation.** Labor costs go up as more food preparation is done in the restaurant's kitchen.
- **Service.** Labor costs go up as more personalized service is provided.
- **Menu.** As the number of items on a menu increase, so does labor cost.
- **Hours of operation.** Every operation has overhead costs that exist regardless of whether the restaurant is closed or open. As a general rule, as long as additional revenue gained by staying open is greater than the additional cost incurred during that period of time, remaining open is desirable from a financial viewpoint.
- **Weather.** To the extent that a restaurant is unable to adjust staff schedules quickly to accommodate unforeseen changes in the weather, labor cost percents will be impacted.
- **Competent management.** The cost of labor is always affected by management's ability to plan, organize, control, direct, and lead the organization in such a way that the desired level of employee performance is obtained at the appropriate level of cost. Good management will have positive effects on labor costs.

4.   Because of the many differences that are readily apparent from one establishment to another within this vast industry, it is impossible to arrive at industrywide standards or averages for a particular manager to use as guides for his or her own establishment. The impact of each of the factors discussed above varies considerably from one establishment to another.

Indeed, two identical restaurants located in different areas do not and probably should not have the same labor costs or the same labor cost percentages. In fact, two such restaurants will normally be found to have significantly different cost structures for food, beverages, and overhead, as well as for labor.

5.   To the inexperienced, labor cost control is sometimes mistakenly taken to suggest the mere reduction of payroll costs to their irreducible minimum. This can be achieved by employing a bare minimum number of people paid the minimum wage. But there is much more to labor cost control than just minimizing dollar wages, a fact sometimes ignored by owners and managers who take the

short-term view of operations, thinking only of immediate profits and not taking into account the long-term effects of their policies and actions.

6. Labor cost control is a process used by managers to direct, regulate, and restrain employees' actions in order to obtain desired levels of performance at appropriate levels of cost. The primary purpose of labor control is to maximize the efficiency of the labor force in a manner consistent with the established standards of quality and service.

The labor cost control process consists of the four control steps: establish standards and standard procedures, train employees, monitor performance and compare actual performance with established standards, and take appropriate action to correct deviations from standards.

IV. KEY TERMS

Following are the key terms discussed in the chapter. It is very important to know these terms and their definitions so you can use them correctly in discussions and in further reading and study. Use the blank spaces to write in definitions.

Bonus

Commission

Compensation

Control process

Current compensation

Deferred compensation

Direct compensation

Directly variable cost

Fixed cost

Gratuities

133

Indirect compensation

Labor cost control

Labor turnover rate

Minimum wage

Salary

Semivariable cost

Tips

Wages

V. SELF-TEST

<u>MATCHING</u>

	TERMS	DEFINITIONS
_____ 1.	Tips	a. Dollar amounts calculated as percentages of sales.
_____ 2.	Wages	b. Fixed dollar amount of compensation.
_____ 3.	Bonus	c. Compensation based on the amount of hours worked.
_____ 4.	Commissions	d. Gratuities.
_____ 5.	Salary	e. Dollar amounts given as a reward.

<u>MULTIPLE CHOICE</u>

6. Bonuses are examples of:
a. Direct compensation.
b. Indirect compensation.
c. Deferred compensation.
d. Future compensation.

7. Free living accommodations is an example of:
a. Direct compensation.
b. Indirect compensation.
c. Deferred compensation.
d. Future compensation.

8. Which of the following is NOT a determinant of total labor costs?
a. Training.
b. Use of outside services.
c. Job specification.
d. Weather.

9. The minimum wage is the:
a. least gross dollar amount that an employer must pay an employee.
b. least net dollar amount that an employer must pay an employee.
c. amount paid to all restaurant employees.
d. amount that is taxed.

10. Compared to other industries, the labor turnover rate in foodservice is:
a. high.
b. low.
c. average.
d. it varies.

11. Labor turnover rate refers to the ratio between the number of:
a. employees who successfully complete the probationary period and those who don't.
b. applicants interviewed for positions to the number hired.
c. departing employees to the total number of employees on staff.
d. departing employees to the number of job classifications.

12. Proper employee training results in:
a. neutral employee morale.
b. reduced labor turnover rate.
c. increased labor costs.
d. employees who take their skills elsewhere.

13. The presence of labor contracts usually means that employee wages are:
a. higher than if there were no union.
b. lower than if there were no union.
c. similar to no union being present.
d. it varies.

14. Which restaurant would most likely have the highest labor cost?
a. fast-food.
b. coffee shop.
c. cafeteria.
d. white tablecloth restaurant with French service and an extensive menu.

15. Which determinant of labor cost is the most noncontrollable?
a. Competent management.
b. Weather.
c. Hours of operation.
d. Labor legislation.

ESSAY/PROBLEMS

16. What's the difference between direct and indirect compensation and between current and deferred compensation?

17. The local pizzeria has a hard time keeping employees for more than a few months. Their labor turnover rate is high, about 250%. What are some hidden costs of the high turnover rate?

18. Discuss how the determinants of labor cost affected the labor cost of a foodservice operation in which you have worked or of a restaurant in your area with which you are familiar.

19. What is labor cost control? Describe the control steps in the labor cost control process.

20. Determine the semivariable cost given the following income statement and a profit of $40,000.

Sales $320,000
Fixed costs   100,000
Directly variable costs 110,000

Chapter 19
ESTABLISHING PERFORMANCE STANDARDS

I. LEARNING OBJECTIVES

Refer to these learning objectives while you are reading the chapter. They will help you focus in on the important points discussed in the chapter. Think of the learning objectives as questions that you will answer while reading the chapter.

1. Explain the meaning and significance of quality and quantity standards in labor control.
2. Identify the three steps used to establish standards and standard procedures for employees.
3. Explain the need for an organizational plan.
4. Describe an organization chart.
5. Define the phrase job description.
6. Define the phrase job analysis, and explain its importance in developing job descriptions.
7. Identify the three parts of a job description.
8. Define the phrase job specification, and explain its importance in making employment decisions.
9. Explain the difference between variable-cost personnel and fixed-cost personnel.
10. Explain how records of business volume are used in scheduling.
11. Explain the difference between the scheduling of variable-cost personnel and the scheduling of fixed-cost personnel.
12. Describe how to prepare an hourly schedule for variable-cost personnel using records of business volume.
13. Describe how to develop performance standards based on a test period.
14. Explain how to determine appropriate staffing levels for an establishment given a table of standard staffing requirements and a sales forecast.

II. CHAPTER OUTLINE

Following are the key headings from this chapter. The purpose of this outline is to help you organize the chapter's main topics. It is also designed to allow you to write key points about each topic in the blank spaces provided. While you are reading the chapter, be sure to take notes using this outline and you will certainly gain a better understanding of the chapter.

1. Introduction

2. Establishing Standards and Standard Procedures

        A. Quality Standards

        B. Quantity Standards

3. Organizing the Enterprise

    A. Establishing an Organizational Plan

    B. Preparing an Organization Chart

4. Preparing Job Descriptions

    A. Job Analysis

    B. Job Descriptions

    C. Job Specifications

5. Scheduling Employees

    A. Labor Classifications for Control Purposes

- Variable Cost Personnel

- Fixed Cost Personnel

    B. Keeping and Using Records of Business Volume

- Daily Tallies

- Hourly Tallies

    C. Developing Schedules for Employees

- Variable Cost Employees

- Fixed Cost Employees

6. Performance Standards Based on Test Period

    A. Variable Cost Personnel

    B. Fixed Cost Personnel

7. Standard Staffing Requirements

8. Standard Work Hours

9. Standard Costs

III. KEY IDEAS

1. The three kinds of standards used in labor cost control are the same used in cost control: quality, quantity, and cost. Before developing quality standards for employee performance, a manager must first have in mind a clear and detailed understanding of the establishment, which includes comprehension of the quality standards for food and beverage products.

Once appropriate quality standards have been established, corresponding quantity standards must be developed. The manager must determine the number of times that a task can be performed within a certain time period at a given level of quality. In effect, the manager must determine the quantity of performance to be expected per hour, per meal, and per day from employees in each job classification. Some fast-food operators have been able to take advantage of production techniques used in typical manufacturing enterprises and have used time and motion studies and other related techniques to establish quantity standards. However, the majority of foodservice operators are not able to use these assembly line techniques. In our industry, other ways must be found to establish quantity standards.

2. Establishing standards and standard procedures for employees requires organizing the enterprise, preparing job descriptions, and scheduling employees.

3. Few activities designed ultimately to control labor cost can be undertaken sensibly until management has devoted appropriate time, thought, and energy to organizing the operation, establishing jobs, and identifying the relationships between them. Organizing an enterprise properly normally requires that one design a rational organizational plan. Establishing an organizational plan requires the owner or manager to first develop a clear picture of the nature of the operation.

4. An organization chart shows the positions and describes reporting relationships within an organization. The lines drawn from one position to another signify the lines of authority. An unbroken line from one position to another indicates that the person below reports to and takes direction from the person immediately above on the chart. The dotted lines show communication and cooperation between the two positions, but one does not have authority over or the responsibility for the actions of the other. Lateral dotted lines show that the two are expected to cooperate in every possible way in accomplishing their respective tasks, but that neither takes direction from the other.

5. A job description is a formal definition of a job, which typically includes a summary of the work to be done and a list of specific tasks and duties. Job descriptions are used to inform employees of their duties and for developing training plans.

Job descriptions should explain what is to be done, as well as when and where. A job description typically has three parts: a heading with job title and department and other pertinent information, a summary of the duties, and a list of the specific duties assigned to the job. Job duties are not only helpful to the employee but also to managers.

6.   Job analysis is the process of identifying the nature of a job as well as the skills, level of education, and other specific qualifications needed to perform the job. It is the first step in

preparing a job description.

The two most common methods of job analysis are interviewing workers and supervisors to obtain the information and observing workers as they perform the jobs. The interviews and observations are designed to provide information about the following.

- Job objectives
- Specific tasks required to achieve objectives
- Performance standards
- Knowledge and skills necessary
- Education and experience required

The manager must also have thorough knowledge of the standards and standard procedures established.

7. Job specifications outline the qualifications needed to perform a job. It is the second outcome of job analysis. A job specification describes the specific skills needed for a given job and the kinds and levels of education and experience required. It is therefore important when making employment decisions.

8. It is important for any manager attempting to develop schedules for employees and to control labor costs to recognize that there are two classifications of employees: variable cost and fixed cost personnel.

Variable cost personnel are those who numbers are linked to business volume. Typical examples of variable cost employees are servers and busboys. As business volume increases, so does the volume of work for these employees.

Fixed cost personnel are those whose numbers are unrelated to business volume. Typical examples include managers, bookkeepers, chefs, and stewards.

9. One very important step that managers should take before scheduling employees is to keep records of business volume. Daily tallies of number of covers served can be prepared from a sales history, guest checks, or electronic cash register. With data collected over a judicious period, business volume can be forecasted with some reasonable degree of accuracy.

Daily records can help control labor cost by enabling the manager to schedule employees' workdays and days off in accordance with anticipated needs. However, it does not help with problems posed by hourly fluctuations in demand. If management develops hourly records of business volume, improved scheduling is possible.

10. A preliminary step in the scheduling of variable cost employees is determining the types and

numbers of employees needed at given levels of business volume. These are used to develop staffing tables. Staffing tables for variable cost employees are estimates of the numbers of these employees required at various levels of business volume, given the quality and quantity standards established for their work. Determining the number of employees required at various levels of business volume is typically an intuitive process based on a manager's experience.

Before fixed cost personnel can be scheduled with any degree of certainty, the manager must determine the specific requirements of the job that should be taken into account in scheduling. When all such requirements have been considered, a manager can establish and post a schedule for fixed cost personnel.

11. With records available of the daily and hourly volume of business and with staffing tables developed from those records, a manager is suitably equipped to schedule variable cost employees. When developing staffing tables, managers must make judgments about the number needed in each job classification affected by hourly volume. For servers, he or she must determine the number of covers that each can serve in a given hour while maintaining the established service standards. Once complete, a schedule would be posted for employees so that each would know his or her scheduled work hours for the coming week.

12. Performance standards developed from records kept during a test period take both quantity and quality standards for work into account. A test period of a particular number of days or weeks is established for gathering data. During this period, detailed sales records are kept, indicating the number of covers served per day or per meal, depending on the type of establishment being analyzed. Management also records the number of staff members on duty in each fixed and variable cost job and reviews each, making judgments about sufficiency of staff and efficiency of employee performance.

13. Once appropriate charts have been prepared for a test period and the manager has a record of sales volume, numbers of variable cost employees working, and his or her own personal estimates of the employees' efficiency, it is time to take the next logical step: to develop a table of standard staffing requirements for variable cost personnel at several levels of business volume.

By judging performance carefully and recording these judgments over a period of time, a manager can set standards for staffing. Referring to these tables of standard labor requirements and to forecasts of anticipated sales for a coming week, the manager can establish better control over labor cost by scheduling the number of personnel necessary to meet the standards of the establishment.

14. Standard work hours are the number of employee work hours required to perform a given volume of work, such as the number of server hours to serve a certain number of customers. Management can develop tables of standard work hours for all job categories at various levels of business activity.

The development of standard work hours makes possible the development of standard labor costs. This may be done by simply multiplying the number of standard work hours required to perform a given volume of work by the hourly wage paid those performing the work.

IV. KEY TERMS

Following are the key terms discussed in the chapter. It is very important to know these terms and their definitions so you can use them correctly in discussions and in further reading and study. Use the blank spaces to write in definitions.

Fixed cost personnel

Job analysis

Job description

Job specification

Median

Organization chart

Organizational plan

Performance criteria

Standard labor cost

Standard staffing requirements

Standard work hours

Variable cost personnel

V. SELF-TEST

MATCHING

	TERMS	DEFINITIONS
_____ 1.	Job analysis	a. Outlines the qualifications needed to perform a job.
_____ 2.	Job description	b. The process of identifying the nature of a job as well as the skills, level of education, and other requirements.
_____ 3.	Performance criteria	c. A document that shows the reporting relationships among positions within an organization.
_____ 4.	Job specification	d. Written statements describing the minimum level of performance acceptable for a job.
_____ 5.	Organization chart	e. A formal definition of a job.

MULTIPLE CHOICE

6. The first step in preparing job descriptions is to:
a. develop performance criteria.
b. come up with job titles.
c. do a job analysis.
d. take corrective steps.

7. _____ personnel are those whose numbers are unrelated to business volume.
a. Fixed cost.
b. Variable cost.
c. Part-time.
d. Full-time.

8. Which of the following is an example of variable cost personnel?
a. A server.
b. A manager.
c. A steward.
d. A bookkeeper.

9. Which of the following is an example of fixed cost personnel?
a. A bellhop.
b. A dishwasher.
c. A chef.
d. A busboy.

10. Business volume is best analyzed on a:
a. daily and hourly basis.
b. daily and weekly basis.
c. weekly and monthly basis.
d. monthly and yearly basis.

11. What is the most accurate method of determining the number of covers served daily?
a. Require the host/hostess to count and record the number.
c. Ask servers to keep records.
b. Use an electronic cash register.
d. Ask cooks to keep accurate production sheets.

12. Schedules for variable cost personnel:
a. are permanent.
c. should be posted one month in advance.
b. tend not to change much from one week to the next.
d. vary with sales volume.

13. If 6 servers are needed to serve 360 covers in three hours, how many standard work hours are required?
a. 6.
c. 18.
b. 10.
d. 300.

14. The development of standard work hours makes possible the development of:
a. standard labor costs.
c. sales forecasts.
b. payroll checks.
d. standard employee schedules.

15. The median is:
a. the average.
c. the mean.
b. the middle point.
d. the hourly volume of business.

ESSAY/PROBLEMS

16. What are the steps used to establish standards and standard procedures for personnel?

17. What is the difference between a dotted and unbroken line on an organization chart?

18. Write up a job description for a position you have had.

19. How is the scheduling of fixed cost and variable cost personnel different?

20. What is meant by standard work hours?

Chapter 20
TRAINING STAFF

I. LEARNING OBJECTIVES

Refer to these learning objectives while you are reading the chapter. They will help you focus in on the important points discussed in the chapter. Think of the learning objectives as questions that you will answer while reading the chapter.

1. Define training, and explain the difference between training and education.
2. Identify the objectives of training.
3. Explain the relationship of training needs assessment to the development of a training plan.
4. List and explain the 10 elements commonly covered in a training plan.
5. Describe the advantages and disadvantages of centralized and local training for multiunit organizations.
6. Identify the four content areas normally included in training manuals.

II. CHAPTER OUTLINE

Following are the key headings from this chapter. The purpose of this outline is to help you organize the chapter's main topics. It is also designed to allow you to write key points about each topic in the blank spaces provided. While you are reading the chapter, be sure to take notes using this outline and you will certainly gain a better understanding of the chapter.

1. Introduction

2. A Definition of Training

3. The Purpose of Training

        A. Training Needs Assessment

        B. Developing Training Plans

            • Objectives

        C. Approaches to Training

            • On-the-job vs. Off-the-job

            • Structured vs. Unstructured

            • Individual vs. Group

            • Training Methods

- Lecture/Demonstration

- Role Playing

- Seminars

- Individual Assignments

- Field Trips

- Case Studies

- Panels

- Programmed Instruction

- Instructional Timetables

- Locations

D. Lesson Plans

- Trainer Preparation

- Trainee Preparation

- The Training Session(s)

- Evaluation

4. Centralized vs. Localized Training

5. Training Manuals

III. KEY IDEAS

1. Training is a process by means of which individuals acquire the skills necessary to perform particular tasks. Training is narrowly focused on particular skills and tasks. It normally includes some education, but it is not the same as education, which is a broader-based term. The objectives of education include increasing one's knowledge of a given subject and developing the capacity of the mind to address complex topics and to analyze critically.

2. The primary purpose of training is to improve job performance. Training is considered a positive factor in achieving organizational and personal goals. Training requires time and money, so one must take care to develop an approach that will meet the needs of the organization.

3. Training starts with a needs assessment that takes a look at present staff and new staff. For present staff members, one should be concerned about their current ability to carry out their tasks and to meet the standards and standard procedures established for their jobs, as well as any future changes that will require additional training. Another consideration for some employers is the extent of the need to institute cross training to enable job rotation. Training is generally required, in well-managed organizations, of all new employees because every foodservice has its own standards and procedures.

4. A training plan is a series of elements that constitute a method for teaching a specific employee the skills required to perform a job correctly and in the manner anticipated by management when the standards and standard procedures for the job were developed. The elements most commonly included are the following.

- Training objectives. Training objectives identify the skills, tasks, and behaviors that a specific employee will have mastered by the time training is complete.
- Approaches to training. Training can be done on the job or off the job. On-the-job training is more commonly used with experienced workers who need only to be shown the methods used by the hospitality operation.
- Training may be done on a structured or an unstructured basis. Structured training is characterized by a formal approach to instruction and may include lesson plans and training films. Unstructured training is commonly undertaken with relatively little thought being given to the specifics of the training. It is often characterized by a trainee being directed to follow and carefully observe an experienced worker doing the job.
- Training can also be done on an individual basis or in groups. Individual training is the most effective, but also the most costly.
- Training methods. There are a number of training methods available: lecture/demonstration, role playing, individual assignments, field trips, seminars, case studies, panels, or programmed instruction. One must select the method(s) that can best be employed for achieving the training objectives established.
- Instructional timetables. Provision for the development of suitable instructional timetables is a major requirement in training plans.
- Locations. Training locations should be determined by the nature of the training to be done. For instance to train servers, some training could take place in the dining room, some training may be more appropriate in a classroom.
- Lesson plans. A lesson plan is a written, step-by-step description of the training required for a specific job, including an objective, detailed notes about content, the instructional timetable, and any items that may be required during instruction. Ideally the lesson plan will be so complete and detailed that any qualified trainer will be able to follow it and deliver the necessary instruction to some individual or group.
- Trainer preparation. At this point, it becomes the responsibility of the trainer to make sure that all is ready for training to begin. Lesson plans must be reviewed. Arrangements must be made for individual employees to be available for training at specific times. Training materials must be gathered and the training site prepared, if necessary.

- Trainee preparation. Trainees should have communicated to them the objectives of the training, the instructional method to be used, and the skills they will learn.
- The training session (s). Good trainers will respond to employees' questions, proceed at a reasonable pace, help trainees feel at ease, speak clearly, use words and phrases appropriate to the language level of the trainees, correct helpfully, and praise appropriately for good work.
- Evaluation. After training of any kind, it is important to evaluate the training, to see if established training objectives have been met and to learn whether those trained are able to meet the performance criteria for their positions. Unless their training has taken place in an entirely realistic work environment, one cannot fully evaluate the future ability of trainees during training. Employees cannot be fully evaluated until they take their places in the workforce, working alongside others.

5. Many multi-unit organizations employ professional human resources personnel to develop training programs that can be implemented throughout the organization. Centralized training at the national or regional headquarters is more common for management personnel. It is a good choice when numerous individuals in various locations all require the same training. Rather than send the trainer on a tour of the locations to provide costly one-on-one training to numerous individuals, it is quicker and probably less expensive to bring all those needing the training to one central location to receive their training together.

Local training at the individual units is a good choice when many individuals in a single unit all require the same training. It is clearly less costly to send one trainer to the unit than to send all the employees to a distant training location.

6. Many large organizations also employ human resources professionals to develop training manuals for use throughout the organization. These can be used any time training is required, regardless of whether the training is done centrally or locally. Training manuals may be written as guides for trainers or are designed to give the trainee the information required even if there is no trainer available to provide instruction. Most training manuals try to include information that can be categorized into these four areas.

1.) General background. The manual should include some introduction to the organization, to its principal goals and objectives, to its philosophy, and to its view of the role of the individual within the organization. In addition it should provide some introduction to the specific job.
2.) Specific duties of a job as well as the performance criteria.
3.) Specific (standard) procedures for carrying out the duties.
4.) Summary. This section normally reemphasizes critical points made earlier, including the importance of the job, major duties, and specific and distinctive standard procedures that render the proper performance of the job critical in the organization.

IV. KEY TERMS

Following are the key terms discussed in the chapter. It is very important to know these terms and their definitions so you can use them correctly in discussions and in further reading and study. Use the blank spaces to write in definitions.

Centralized training

Cross training

Job rotation

Localized training

On-the-job training

Off-the-job training

Training

Training manual

Training objectives

Training plan

V. SELF-TEST

MATCHING

	TERM	DEFINITION
_____ 1.	On-the-job training	a. Training at a central training facility.
_____ 2.	Off-the-job training	b. Training while the employee is performing the actual job.
_____ 3.	Cross training	c. Training at the normal work site or close by.
_____ 4.	Centralized training	d. Teaching an employee to perform the duties of another position.
_____ 5.	Localized training	e. Training an employee away from the work area.

MULTIPLE CHOICE

6. Training and education are:
a. the same.
b. different: education is a broader-based term.
c. different: training is a broader-based term.
d. different: education only occurs in schools.

7. New employees need:
a. orientation.
b. evaluation.
c. cross training.
d. learner objectives.

8. Which is NOT an element of training plans?
a. Objectives.
b. Location.
c. Trainee preparation.
d. Layout.

9. On-the-job training is more commonly used with:
a. employees with few foodservice skills.
b. experienced workers.
c. both experienced and inexperienced employees.
d. work that can't be easily monitored and corrected.

10. Which is NOT a training method?
a. Role playing.
b. Panels.
c. Three-sink method.
d. Programmed instruction.

11. A handbook that provides for standardized training directed towards standardized results is a:
a. lesson plan.
b. training plan.
c. training objective.
d. training manual.

12. Adults learn best when:

a. they are treated like kids in school.

b. they understand the need for learning.

c. there is some apprehension.

d. training sessions are long.

13. Training _____ identify the skills, tasks, and behaviors that a specific employee will have mastered by the time training is completed.

a. approaches.

b. methods.

c. objectives.

d. sessions.

14. Individual training can most easily be accomplished by:

a. programmed instruction.

b. field trips.

c. role playing.

d. panels.

ESSAY/PROBLEMS

15. What are some of the benefits of training employees?

16. In a previous or current job, describe the training you received.

17. For which employees might job rotation be helpful?

18. What are the parts of a lesson plan?

19. What should be done to prepare trainees for training?

20. How can training be evaluated and why?

Chapter 21
MONITORING PERFORMANCE AND TAKING CORRECTIVE ACTION

I. LEARNING OBJECTIVES

Refer to these learning objectives while you are reading the chapter. They will help you focus in on the important points discussed in the chapter. Think of the learning objectives as questions that you will answer while reading the chapter.

1. Define the term monitoring as it is used in labor cost control.
2. Explain the difference between direct and indirect monitoring of employee performance.
3. Identify the two types of direct monitoring and provide examples of each.
4. List and describe four sources of information used for indirect monitoring.
5. Identify the five-step approach used to identify the specific cause of some deviation between actual and standard performance.
6. List and describe the three general causes of discrepancies between actual performance and that anticipated by standards.

II. CHAPTER OUTLINE

Following are the key headings from this chapter. The purpose of this outline is to help you organize the chapter's main topics. It is also designed to allow you to write key points about each topic in the blank spaces provided. While you are reading the chapter, be sure to take notes using this outline and you will certainly gain a better understanding of the chapter.

1. Introduction

2. Monitoring Performance

      A. Direct Monitoring

      B. Indirect Monitoring

            • Customers

            • Employees

            • External Agencies/Organizations/Groups

                  1. Government Agencies

                  2. Chain Organizations

                  3. Food Critics

4. Rating Organizations

- Managers

3. Taking Corrective Action

       A. Inadequate Performance

       B. Unsuitable Standards

       C. Inappropriate Organization

III. KEY IDEAS

1. To monitor the performance of employees is to gather information about their work and the results of that work. This is the necessary third step in the control process - the step that enables management to make those judgments about performance that will suggest whether or not corrective action will be required.

2. Direct monitoring of employee performance normally means direct observation by a manager of an employee at work or direct examination of the results of that employee's work. Indirect monitoring of employees' performance refers to informal procedures by means of which managers obtain information about operations without directly observing those operations.

3. Direct monitoring may involve directly observing an employee attending to a task or examining the results of their work and making a judgment about it immediately after it has been done.

4. The sources that provide the information needed for indirect monitoring include customers, employees, external groups (such as government agencies, chain organization inspectors, food critics, and rating organizations), and managers.

Customer complaints or compliments may be verbal or written. When reports from employees about their co-workers come to supervisors, it is important that they be carefully considered. Government agencies include local fire departments, health and safety inspectors from a Health Department or from OSHA, or inspections carried out by representatives of any number of other agencies. Managers at all levels may be the most important of those engaged in monitoring the performance levels of staff.

5. If actual performance brings results that deviate significantly from those anticipated by established standards and standard procedures, some corrective action must be taken to bring actual performance into line with the standards. There is a generally accepted five-step approach that can be used to identify the cause and find a suitable solution.

       1. Meet with appropriate staff to point out the problems and determine its cause.
       2. Identify all appropriate corrective measures that might be adopted.
       3. Select the best corrective measure.

4. Institute the selected measure.

5. Monitor performance to be sure that corrective measure has the desired effect.

6. There are three possible reasons for discrepancies between actual performance and that anticipated by standards. They include: inadequate performance, unsuitable standards, and inappropriate organization.

IV. KEY TERMS

Following are the key terms discussed in the chapter. It is very important to know these terms and their definitions so you can use them correctly in discussions and in further reading and study. Use the blank spaces to write in definitions.

Direct monitoring

Indirect monitoring

Monitoring

Reorganization

Standards

Standard procedures

V. SELF-TEST

MULTIPLE CHOICE

1. Asking customers about their meal and service is an example of:

a. direct monitoring.

b. indirect monitoring.

c. corrective action.

d. problem-solving.

2. If there is a discrepancy between actual performance and that anticipated by standards and standard procedures, it might be due to:

a. inadequate performance.

b. unsuitable standards.

c. inappropriate organization.

d. all of the above.

3. Who is probably the most important of those engaged in monitoring the performance levels of staff?

a. Customers.

b. Government agencies.

c. Managers.

d. Other employees.

4. Many foodservice chains employ _____ to perform a monitoring service by visiting and scrutinizing units.

a. food critics.

b. inspectors.

c. sanitarians.

d. dietitians.

5. When performance deviates significantly from that anticipated by established standards and standard procedures:

a. corrective action is needed.

b. discipline should be instituted.

c. performance needs to be watched until it improves.

d. indirect monitoring is needed.

ESSAY/PROBLEMS

6. Describe direct and indirect monitoring, giving examples of how each is done.

7. Although plating standards require appropriate garnishes on every entree plate, as the manager, you have noticed lately that garnishes are only being used on some plates. Describe the five-step approach you would use to correct this performance.

8. List three government agencies that may be found inspecting food and beverage operations.

9. What are three possible reasons for discrepancies between actual performance and that anticipated by standards?

Study Guide Solutions

Chapter 1 -- Cost and Sales Concepts

1. c
3. a
5. i
7. h
9. g

11. c
13. c
15. a
17. c
19. c

21. 28.1%
     31.7%

23. Raw dollar figures for costs are seldom, if ever, of any particular significance for control purposes. Because these costs vary to some extent with business volume, they become significant only when expressed in relation to that volume with which they vary. Foodservice managers calculate costs in dollars and compare those costs to sales in dollars. This enables them to discuss the relationship between cost to sales or the cost-to-sales ratio.

25. See income statement in text.

Chapter 2 -- The Control Process

1. c
3. h
5. a
7. d
9. f

11. b
13. d
15. b
17. b
19. a

21. While cost control is very important to the profitable operation of any business, it alone will not ensure profitability. Additional steps must be taken to ensure that all sales result in appropriate income to the business. For example, profits will be adversely affected if a steak listed in the menu for $18.95 is sold to a customer for $15.95.

23. The control process consists of four steps.
     Establish standards and standard procedures for operation.
     Train all individuals to follow established standards and standard procedures.
     Monitor performance and compare actual performances with established standards.
     Take appropriate action to correct deviations from standards.

25. Budget for Continental Restaurant

Sales		
	Food	$380
	Beverage	$80
	Total Sales	$460
Cost of Sales		
	Food	$140,600
	Beverage	$20,000
	Total	$160,600
	Gross Profit	$299,400
Controllable Expenses		
	Fixed Salaries and Wages	$40,000
	Variable Salaries and Wages	$76,000
	Employee Benefits	$27,840
	Other Controllable Expenses	$55,000
	Total	$198,840
Income Before Occupancy Costs		$100,560
Income Before Occupancy Costs		$33,000
Occupancy Costs		
Income Before Interest and Depreciation		$67,560
Interest		$4,500
Depreciation		$23,000
Restaurant Profit		$40,060

Chapter 3 -- Cost/Volume/Profit Relationships

1. d   9. d
3. g   11. d
5. h   13. b
7. c

15. $6.20
17. 57
19. $180,000
21. $9,750

Chapter 4 -- Food Purchasing and Receiving Controls

1. c   17. b
3. a   19. c
5. i   21. c
7. d   23. d
9. e   25. c
11. b   27. a
13. d   29. d

15. c

31.   Reorder point is 30 cans. Reorder quantity is 38 cans or 3 cases.

33.   Under a centralized purchasing system, the requirements of individual units are relayed to a central office, which determines total requirements of all units and then purchases that total. Some advantages of this system including purchasing at lower prices (because of the high volume), obtaining the exact specifications, and fewer possibilities for dishonest purchasing. Disadvantages include less buying freedom for the unit to purchase for its own peculiar needs and restraining the individual unit manager's freedom to change a menu.

35.   It is generally good practice to provide the receiving clerk with an invoice stamp - a rubber stamp to be used on all invoices. This stamp is used for a number of reasons. It provides for:

- Verification of the date on which food was received.
- The signature of the clerk receiving the food who vouches for the accuracy of quantities, qualities, and prices.
- The steward's signature, indicating the steward knows the food has been delivered.
- The food controller's verification of the arithmetical accuracy of the bill.
- Signatory approval of the bill for payment by an authorized individual before a check is drawn.

37.   Deliveries should be made when each can be given the proper amount of attention to be received properly.

Chapter 5 -- Food Storing and Issuing Controls

1. b   7. c
3. e   9. b
5. d

11.   FIFO is the procedure used to ensure that older quantities of any item are used before any new deliveries. New deliveries are stored behind the quantities already on hand.

13.   Security is an important consideration in the case of high-cost items such as meat, fish, and liquor.

15. $21.05

Chapter 6 -- Food Production Control I: Portions

1. d   11. c
3. g   13. d
5. f   15. b
7. c   17. c
9. b   19. c

21.   a. $5.94
       b. $7.79
23. $1.83
25.   Yield factor: .55
       Standard Portion Cost: $3.06

Portion Cost Factor: 0.68
Pound Cost Factor: 1.80

Chapter 7 -- Food Production Control II: Quantities

1. b   7. b
3. d   9. c
5. c

11.   A 28.4%
       B 17.0%
       C 11.3%
       D 22.7%
       E 20.6%
13.   A 66
       B 39
       C 26
       D 52
       E 47

15.   Every restaurant offering steaks, chops, and other similar a la carte entrees has had some experience with portions being rejected by customers and returned from the dining room for one reason or another. There are also many occasions when portions are returned because some member of the staff was not listening or made another similar mistake. These returned portions are excellent examples of excessive cost and should not be ignored.

       Whenever a portion is returned, some authorized individual records it on the void sheet, indicating the name of the item, the number of the check on which it appeared, and the reason for its return. These entries can be most revealing to an alert manager or food controller.

Chapter 8 -- Monitoring Foodservice Operations I: Monthly Inventory and Monthly Food Costs

1. i   11. d
3. e   13. c
5. b   15. c
7. h   17. b
9. c   19. d

21. $11,812
23.   Food cost percent: 45.4%
       Food cost per dollar sale: $0.454

Chapter 9 -- Monitoring Foodservice Operations II: Daily Food Costs

1. b   7. a
3. e   9. a
5. a

11. 6/15 Food Cost: $310
          Food Cost Percent Today: 25.8%
     6/16 Food Cost: $365
          Food Cost Percent Today: 24.3%
          Food Cost Percent To Date: 25%
13. Difference is $579.56.

Chapter 10 -- Monitoring Foodservice Operations III: Actual Versus Standard Food Cost

1. d   7. b
3. b   9. b
5. c

11. Reasons for differences between standard and actual costs could include overpurchasing, overproduction, pilferage, spoilage, improper portioning, and failure to follow standard recipes.
13. a. $1,229.50
     b. $523.85
     c. 44.7%
     d. 42.6%
     e. $26.15 or 2.1% of sales

Chapter 11 -- Menu Analysis

1. b   7. b
3. d   9. a
5. a

Chapter 12 -- Food Sales Control

1. b   9. c
3. e   11. d
5. a   13. b
7. a   15. c

17. Students' responses will vary.
19. The five most important elements of menu preparation are as follows.
     1. Layout and design - The entire physical menu (the paper, the color, the printing, and so on) should suit the character and style of the restaurant.
     2. Variety - There should be a variety of foods and menu prices.
     3. Item arrangement and location - The items management wants to really sell should be the featured items – the items in greatest supply in the kitchen and with the most favorable cost-to-sales ratio. Items listed first and at the top of a list are seen first and make the greatest impression.
     4. Descriptive language - The descriptions of foods may increase sales.
     5. Kitchen personnel and equipment - Anyone writing a menu should have a clear, unbiased

view of the culinary abilities of present staff.

Chapter 13 -- Beverage Purchasing Control

1. c	11. b
3. g	13. c
5. h	15. a
7. a	17. a
9. i	19. b

21.   The primary purposes of beverage purchasing controls are:
1. To maintain an appropriate supply of ingredients for producing beverage products.
2. To ensure that the quality of ingredients purchased are appropriate to intended use.
3. To ensure that ingredients are purchased at optimum prices.

23. To process orders, it is advisable to establish a purchasing routine that requires formal written purchase orders. In a large hotel, the purchasing routine might be the following: a wine steward, as the person in charge of maintaining the beverage inventory and stockroom, would prepare a purchase request in duplicate just after the first of the month. The original would go to the purchasing agent who would write up a purchase order. One copy of the purchase order would go to the receiving clerk so that he or she would know what deliveries to expect and be able to receive them properly.

25.

Item	Par Stock	Reorder Point	Reorder Quantity
Scotch	63	23	55
Rum	42	15	37

Chapter 14 -- Beverage Receiving, Storing, and Issuing Control

1. b	9. c
3. d	11. a
5. c	13. b
7. a	

15.   The primary goal of receiving control is to ensure that deliveries received conform exactly to orders placed. In practice, this means that beverage deliveries must be compared to beverage orders with respect to quantity, quality, and price.

Storing control is established in beverage operations to achieve three important objectives: to prevent pilferage, to ensure accessibility when needed, and to preserve quality.

Issuing control is established to achieve two objectives: to ensure the timely release of beverages from inventory in the needed quantities and to prevent the misuse of alcoholic beverages between release from inventory and delivery to the bar.

17.   There are two ways to maintain the necessary degree of security in beverage areas. The first is to assign the responsibility for security of the stored items to one person alone. The second way to maintain security is to keep the beverage storage facility locked and to issue a single key to one person who will be held accountable for all beverages in the inventory. The person with the key would be required to open the lock and issue the needed beverages.

19.   A requisition system is a highly structured method for controlling issues. A key element in the system is the requisition form, on which both the names of beverages the quantities of each issued are recorded. No bottles should ever be issued without a written requisition signed by an authorized person, often the head bartender. The head bartenders usually determines the quantities needed at the bar to replenish the par stock.

After the beverages have been issued, the unit value of each beverage is entered on the requisition, and these individual values are extended.

The majority of establishments take the further precaution of requiring that each requisition from a front bar or a service bar be accompanied by empty bottles from the bar, to ensure that the units issued are actually replacing quantities the bartender has used.

Chapter 15 -- Beverage Production Control

1. e	9. b
3. c	11. d
5. b	13. b
7. d	

15.   Control over beverage production is established to achieve two primary objectives: to ensure that all drinks are prepared according to management's specifications and to guard against excessive costs that can develop in the production process.

In order to achieve these objectives, management must establish appropriate standards. Standards must be established for the quantities of ingredients used in drink preparation as well as for the proportions of ingredients in a drink. In other words, standard recipes must be established so that bar personnel will know the exact quantity of each ingredient to use in order to produce any given drink. In addition, drink sizes must be standardized.

When standards are set for ingredients, proportions, and drink sizes, customers can have some reasonable assurance that a drink will meet expectations each time it is ordered. Management also establishes a means for controlling costs.

17.   One common approach to monitoring beverage production is to observe bartenders as they proceed with their daily work. Observation could be done by a manager, a designated employee such as a head bartender, individuals unknown to the bartenders, or closed-circuit television.

19.   a. $0.82
       b. $1.17

Chapter 16 -- Monitoring Beverage Operations

1. b	9. b
3. d	11. c
5. a	13. b
7. a	15. d

17.   45%
19.   Deviation is $300 or 2.9%, $7,767

164

Chapter 17 -- Beverage Sales Control

1. a
3. e
5. b

7. c
9. b

11.   People may patronize bars and restaurants with bars for any of the following reasons: to socialize, to conduct business, to eat, to seek entertainment, and to waste time.

13. Some poor bartender work habits include:

- working with cash drawer open,
- under-ringing sales,
- overcharging customers,
- undercharging customers,
- overpouring,
- underpouring,
- diluting bottle contents,
- bringing own bottle into the bar,
- charging for drinks not served, and
- drinking on the job.

15.   An automated bar is both an electronic sales terminal and a computerized dispensing device for beverages. The dispensing device is controlled by the sales terminal. When a customer orders a drink, the bartender places the proper glassware under the dispensing device, inserts a guest check in the terminal or in a separate printer controlled by the terminal, and depresses the terminal key with the name of the drink on it.

There are some significant advantages to automated systems over traditional methods of preparing drinks. The proportions of ingredients are exactly the same each time a given drink is prepared, and the drinks are thus of uniform quality, prepared according to the standard recipes programmed; the quantity of each ingredient is measured exactly, and the sizes of all drinks of any given type are uniform. However, it must be noted that these systems only reduce the possibilities for the development of excessive costs through pilferage, spillage, and various bartender errors. The possibilities for charging incorrect prices are greatly reduced.

There are also some important disadvantages to these systems. Most cannot accommodate customers' requests for drinks made according to recipes other than the standard recipes programmed. At front bars, many customers have negative reactions to automated bars. For these customers, having drinks prepared by a machine takes something away from their experience. In addition, traditional methods of drink preparation often give customers the impression that the bartender is giving them more than the standard measure, a dividend, so to speak.

Chapter 18 -- Labor Cost Considerations

1. d
3. e
5. b
7. b

9. a
11. c
13. a
15. b

17.   Some hidden costs of high turnover include management time engaged in recruiting and hiring and lowered employee morale.

19.   Labor cost control is a process used by managers to direct, regulate, and restrain employees' actions in order to obtain desired levels of performance at appropriate levels of cost. The primary purpose of labor control is to maximize the efficiency of the labor force in a manner consistent with the established standards of quality and service.

        The labor cost control process consists of the four control steps: establish standards and standard procedures, train employees, monitor performance and compare actual performance with established standards, and take appropriate action to correct deviations from standards.

Chapter 19 -- Establishing Performance Standards

1. b   9. c
3. d   11. b
5. c   13. c
7. a   15. b

17.   An unbroken line from one position to another indicates that the person below reports to and takes direction from the person immediately above on the chart. The dotted lines show communication and cooperation between the two positions, but one does not have authority over or the responsibility for the actions of the other. Lateral dotted lines show that the two are expected to cooperate in every possible way in accomplishing their respective tasks, but that neither takes direction from the other.

19.   A preliminary step in the scheduling of variable cost employees is determining the types and numbers of employees needed at given levels of business volume. These are used to develop staffing tables. Staffing tables for variable cost employees are estimates of the numbers of these employees required at various levels of business volume, given the quality and quantity standards established for their work. Determining the number of employees required at various levels of business volume is typically an intuitive process based on a manager's experience. Before fixed cost personnel can be scheduled with any degree of certainty, the manager must determine the specific requirements of the job that should be taken into account in scheduling.

Chapter 20 -- Training Staff

1. b   9. b
3. d   11. d
5. c   13. c
7. a

15.   Employees who are properly training will be more efficient, enabling management to keep labor costs to their practical minimum. This should result in better financial performance. Properly training employees will e more effective and able to do their jobs in the manner that presents the establishment in its most favorable light. Well-trained employees are more likely to continue working for the employers, thus keeping the labor turnover rate lower.

17.   Job rotation is especially helpful in positions that are more routine and boring.

19.   Trainees should have communicated to them the objectives of the training, the instructional

166

method to be used, and the skills they will learn.

Chapter 21 -- Monitoring Performance and Taking Corrective Action

1. b   5. a
3. c

7.   If actual performance brings results that deviate significantly from those anticipated by established standards and standard procedures, some corrective action must be taken to bring actual performance into line with the standards. There is a generally accepted five-step approach that can be used to identify the cause and find a suitable solution.
    1. Meet with appropriate staff to point out the problems and determine its cause.
    2. Identify all appropriate corrective measures that might be adopted.
    3. Select the best corrective measure.
    4. Institute the selected measure.
    5. Monitor performance to be sure that corrective measure has the desired effect.

9.   There are three possible reasons for discrepancies between actual performance and that anticipated by standards. They include: inadequate performance, unsuitable standards, and inappropriate organization.